SOCIOLOGY IN FOCUS SERIES
General Editor: Murray Morison

Gender

Pat Mayes

LONGMAN
London a

LONGMAN GROUP UK LIMITED
Longman House, Burnt Mill, Harlow, Essex CM20 2JE, UK
and Associated Companies throughout the World.

Published in the United States of America
by Longman Inc., New York

First published 1986
Sixth impression 1992
ISBN 0 582 35496 X

Set in 10/11pt Bembo, Linotron 202

Produced by Longman Singapore Publishers Pte Ltd
Printed in Singapore

British Library Cataloguing in Publication Data

Mayes, Pat
    Gender — (Sociology in focus)
    1. Sex role
    I. Title   II. Series
    305.3   BF692.2

ISBN 0-582-35496-X

Library of Congress Cataloging in Publication Data

Mayes, Pat
    Gender
    (Sociology in focus series)
    Bibliography: p.
    Includes index.
    1. Sex role — Great Britain. 2. Sexual division of
labor — Great Britain. 3. Sex discrimination — Great Britain. I. Title. II. Series.
HQ 1075.5.G7M39 1986   305.3'0941   85-14971
ISBN 0-582-35496-X

Contents

Acknowledgements

Many thanks to Murray for his patient and constructive criticism. Thank you also to my family and friends who showed interest and encouragement. Special love and thanks to Nicky, Jane and Chris for their patience and humour and for the 'bottomless tea-pot'.

To the memory of my sister, Joan.

We are grateful to the following for permission to reproduce copyright material:

the author, C Bell and the Equal Opportunities Commission for an extract from *Fathers, Childbirth and Work* by C Bell, L McKee & K Priestly; Croom Helm Ltd for fig 4.2 & an extract from *The Double Standard: A Feminist Critique of Feminist Social Science* by M Eichler; Economic and Social Research Council and the Equal Opportunities Commission for fig 5.6, table 5 & an extract from *Social Networks and Job Information: the situation of women who return to work* by J Chaney; the author, H Hartman and the University of Chicago Press for fig 5.4 adapted from the article 'Capitalism, Patriarchy and Job Segregation by Sex' in *Signs* Vol 1 No 3 Pt 2; the Controller, Her Majesty's Stationery Office for tables 2a,b,c from *Education of Girls: A Statistical Analysis*, table 6 from *Subject Women* by A Oakley; Hutchinson Publishing Group Ltd for an extract from *Gender and Schooling* by M Stanworth; the author, G P Murdock and the editor for table 10 from table 2.1 *Social Forces* Copyright © The University of North Carolina Press; the author, Dr L Murgatroyd for table 9 & an extract from the paper 'Gender and Occupational Stratification'; Office of Population Censuses and Surveys for fig 5.1 from *General Household Survey* 1980 & table 7 from *New Earnings Survey* 1983 Crown Copyright; The Open University for fig 3.4 & an extract from *Co-Education Reconsidered* ed R Deem © 1984 Open University Press; Routledge & Kegan Paul PLC for fig 2.2 & extracts from *The Sex Role System* by J and E Newson, an extract from *Woman's Worth: Sexual Economics and the World of Women* by L Leghorn & K Parker; Verso Editions for fig 7.2 & table 11 from *Women's Oppression Today* by M Barrett; Virago Press Ltd for fig 7.1 © The Cambridge Women's Studies Group from *Women in Society*; The Women's Press Ltd for fig 3.2 Copyright A Walters & fig 3.3 Copyright M Scott from *Learning to Lose* ed Sarah & Spender; Writers and Readers Publishing Cooperative Society Ltd for table 1 from *Sex Roles in Reading Schemes* by G Lobban.

We are unable to trace the copyright holder in the poem 'Chantefleurs, Chantefables' by R Desnos and would appreciate any information that would enable us to do so.

Series introduction

Sociology in Focus aims to provide an up-to-date, coherent coverage of the main topics that arise on an introductory course in sociology. While the intention is to do justice to the intricacy and complexity of current issues in sociology, the style of writing has deliberately been kept simple. This is to ensure that the student coming to these ideas for the first time need not become lost in what can appear initially as jargon.

Each book in the series is designed to show something of the purpose of sociology and the craft of the sociologist. Throughout the different topic areas the interplay of theory, methodology and social policy have been highlighted, so that rather than sociology appearing as an unwieldy collections of facts, the student will be able to grasp something of the process whereby sociological understanding is developed. The format of the books is broadly the same throughout. Part one provides an overview of the topic as a whole. In part two the relevant research is set in the context of the theoretical, methodological and policy issues. The student is encouraged to make his or her own assessment of the various arguments, drawing on the statistical and reference material provided both here and at the end of the book. The final part of the book contains both statistical material and a number of 'Readings'. Questions have been provided in this section to direct students to analyse the materials presented in terms of both theoretical assumptions and methodological approaches. It is intended that this format should enable students to exercise their own sociological imaginations rather than to see sociology as a collection of universally accepted facts, which just have to be learned.

While each book in the series is complete within itself, the similarity of format ensures that the series as a whole provides an integrated and balanced introduction to sociology. It is intended that the text can be used both for individual and classroom study, while the inclusion of the variety of statistical and documentary materials lend themselves to both the preparation of essays and brief seminars.

Snow Long

PART 1

Introduction and overview

1 Introduction

> According to the book of Genesis, God first created man. Woman was not only an afterthought, but an amenity. For close on two thousand years this holy scripture was believed to justify her subordination and explain her inferiority for even as a copy she was not a very good copy. There were differences. She was not one of his best efforts.
>
> Elaine Morgan, *The Descent of Woman,* Souvenir Press, 1972

> When God made man she was only practising.
>
> Graffiti on the wall of a women's lavatory, 1975

Both these statements (although the first is heavy with irony) illustrate a debate that must seem, to many students, to be a confused, confusing and contradictory argument. Is one sex 'superior' to the other? And if it is, who decides the criteria for superiority? Further, what are the consequences of being a member of the 'inferior' group? This text will attempt to set the argument in context and introduce students to some of the key areas of debate.

By the age of two most children are aware of the primary division of the species into male and female. The differences are clear at birth and become more marked as we mature. The biological differences are decided at the moment of conception and, in all but a very few cases, present a non-controversial issue. The possession of one set of genitals or another clearly predisposes us to one type of activity; at some time in our life we may decide to become a mother or a father. Which of these we become is a matter of biology, not choice. But when the terms 'masculine' or 'feminine' are used and when an individual is described as 'manly' or 'girlish' judgements are being made which are a product of culture, rather than chromosomes. Being born male or female has implications far beyond the possibility of someday being a father or a mother. On the basis of an individual's sex, predictions can be made about areas of his or her life quite remote from their potential parenting activities. It is possible, for example, to estimate their chances of being a patient in a mental hospital, of their being a victim of violence, of their possible educational achievement, and even of their potential earning power.

It is useful to make a distinction between **sex**, a term which will be used to refer to biologically determined features which make us male or female and **gender**, which will be employed to discuss the more debatable issue of how sex differences are translated and interpreted in everyday life. It will be gender that will be examined most as we consider the differences between men's and women's roles, life-chances and experiences, and as we establish the degree to which differentials in power, prestige and status exist between the sexes.

Theoretical approaches to gender

There are some who would argue that sex and gender are inseparable; that, in fact, **Biology is Destiny**. Such theorists argue that individuals are naturally inclined to certain types of activity, that men and women have certain tendencies and abilities (or lack of abilities) which suit them to various roles and occupations. This text will assess the validity of such claims and examine other variables which may contribute to gendered activity.

One way of doing this is to look at other cultures, for if a phenomenon is universal there is a strong possibility that it is natural. After all, whatever the culture, the physiological differences between men and women are the same. However, not all cultures interpret these differences in the same way. Female and male roles vary from culture to culture and there is no universal definition of 'masculinity' or 'femininity'.

Functionalist theory offers a more sophisticated analysis for it allows for cultural variations in gender roles and argues that however a society 'shapes' its men and women into different spheres, those differences can nevertheless be seen as functional to the maintenance of social stability and harmony. It is, after all, quite 'functional' to divide work roles along sex lines, so that women perform domestic tasks and childcare and men provide economic support. However, this theory raises as many problems as the Biology is Destiny argument, for who decides what is best for society and for the men and women within it? Whose vision of society is being accepted and in whose interest is this method of organisation? How does prestige and status come to be attached to one sphere of activity and not another? For example, if the biological mother is seen as best suited to caring for young children, why does she perform these tasks unpaid? If sociologists are to understand gender differences and sex stratification these areas must be opened up for research, explanation and understanding.

Perhaps it is a matter of power? Some theorists suggest that all human relationships are based upon the ability of one group to dominate and control the lives of others.

Contemporary **Marxist theory** attributes the role of women to capitalism and argues that capitalist economies trap men in wage labour and keep women in low-paid work or unpaid domestic labour. More recently, **feminist theory** has suggested that patriarchy – a system of male power and control – colluded with capital and pushed women to the margins of an industrial economy, thereby ensuring that males acquire power, profit and resultant prestige. All these sociological theories require evaluation and their contribution to the understanding of sex differences needs to be assessed.

Structure and ideology

Human beings inherit a culture but each generation re-creates or re-defines part of it. There is certainly evidence that sex roles have changed but there is also evidence that they remain remarkably stable; despite the increasing numbers of women entering paid work there are still many who firmly believe that 'a woman's place is in the home'. There is little evidence to suggest that women's increased participation in paid labour has meant decreased responsibility for childcare and domestic work. Similarly, legislation which ensured equal educational opportunities for girls has not yet brought about any significant change in the numbers of young women entering engineering or scientific and technical spheres of employment.

It is useful, then, to distinguish between the **structural** changes in a society, such as smaller family size or the theoretical possibility of equal opportunities for women, and the **ideological** changes such as the way a culture defines and evaluates the concepts 'maleness' or 'femaleness'. The two examples used earlier may illustrate this further: If married women workers are still expected to be responsible for housework, shopping, cooking and childcare they are unlikely to seek or find a demanding job which pays high wages or leads to professional advancement. If a schoolgirl, choosing her subject options, sees the physics department run by men, dominated by boys and concerned mainly with mechanical concepts which are unfamiliar to her, she is less likely than a boy to choose that subject. To do so may mean entering a sphere which conflicts with her internalised notions of 'feminine' activity. The same, of course, applies to a boy considering domestic science; such a choice may 'de-sex' him in his own and his peers' estimation. So, running contrary to what may or may not be a structural change in the role of women is an ideology of femininity which has been much slower to change. Also running counter to female emancipation is an ideology of masculinity. It may well be that only against a backdrop of female passivity can men remain dominant. A stereotypical high-achieving, successful businessman can probably only reach his exalted position if he has a woman who performs his domestic chores and raises his children.

The history of gender

As key areas of women's lives are examined throughout the text, reference will be made to the juxtaposition of the structure and ideology of sex roles. It may be said that even raising such issues remains a somewhat risky enterprise. Questioning the ideology of gender means questioning an individual's sexual identity. Some people find this very threatening and the response may be hostile; contemporary feminists are not the first to be called 'man haters'. In 1792, Mary Wollstonecraft wrote *A Vindication of the Rights of Women*, described by Kate Millet as 'the feminist declaration of independence'. Walpole, however, denounced Wollstonecraft as 'a hyena in petticoats'. Perhaps the strength of the response is a measure of the challenge feminism presents to the existing order. Any movement which attempts to alter existing power relations has brought abusive, sometimes violent response. Although there is space in this text to describe only the contemporary Women's Movement, the history of women's struggle for justice and equality is a fascinating one, which can be traced in Spender (1983).

The organisation of this book

The next chapter addresses itself to the problem of how a society can take two individuals who differ only in sex, and successfully mould them into the gender role of 'girl' and 'boy'. Chapter 3 considers the role of education in this process.

In Chapters 4 and 5 we try to analyse the relationship between women, marriage and 'work', whether it be in the home or at a place of paid employment.

Chapter 6 takes a slightly broader perspective on women and 'power' in various societies, and Chapter 7 looks at the recent rise of the women's movement and how it has analysed and challenged the structure and ideology of gender.

Throughout the text run two recurrent themes. One is concerned with policy; with trying to clarify what needs to be done, both structurally and ideologically, in order to achieve equality between the sexes. The second raises the issue of social theory and of methodology. It is necessary to question whether current sociological theory, from the various theoretical standpoints outlined earlier in this Introduction, can adequately assess and explain the role of women in society. Indeed, some recent feminist theory has argued that men have constructed theories which reflect and consolidate their own privileged position:

> Born into a society in which their plentiful theories are the framework for making sense of the world (and this includes 'making sense' of women in relation to themselves), men have had their confidence boosted, their assurance reinforced, their authority confirmed.
>
> Dale Spender, *Feminist Theorists*, Women's Press, 1983

That 'authority' has been challenged by recent feminist theory and this text will reflect some of those developments.

A text of this length is heavily dependent on a selection procedure which will inevitably displease some. For example, space has not allowed for detailed discussion of the role of the mass media, religion or the state in the maintenance of gender differences. Interested readers will find references to suitable texts in the bibliography.

PART 2

Sociology and gender

2 Sex-role socialisation

Sex-role socialisation is well-researched but the evidence is often conflicting. This is partly a result of different methodologies. For example, Maccoby and Jacklin (in Lloyd and Archer, *The Psychology of Sex Differences,* 1974) found very few examples of children being openly directed to gender-specific activity in their laboratory observations. However, when Belotti (*Little Girls Social Conditioning and its Effects on Stereotyped Roles,* 1975) undertook participant observations in nursery schools she found many more instances of parents and teachers suggesting gender-appropriate activities. When asked directly, most teachers profess support for equal opportunities, but observation of their classes reveals repeated instances of them treating the sexes quite differently. Children tend to choose gender-appropriate behaviour from about the age of two, and few parents or teachers seem to suggest a wider choice of activity.

Those sociologies which suggest that societies are integrated by its members internalising shared norms and values, argue that sex-role socialisation is necessary to ensure the continuation of social organisation. Thus, Parsons believed that:

> Equality of opportunity (for the sexes) is clearly incompatible with any solidarity of the family. . .Where married women are employed outside the home it is, for the great majority, in occupations which are not in direct competition for the status of those men of their own class. Women's interest and the standard of judgement applied to them run, in our society, far more in the direction of personal adornment.
>
> T. Parsons, *Essays in Social Theory,* Free Press, 1979

According to these criteria then, little girls must be taught domestic skills, to look pretty and to refrain from 'direct competition' with boys. It is necessary, however, to ask who benefits from this type of social organisation. Marxist theorists such as Sue Sharpe argue that women's domestic role benefits capitalism; women perform essential services for the labour force and provide a market-place for the products of private industry.

Problems of perspective and method

Capitalism is the economic backdrop against which children play out their 'practice runs' and learn their roles. Acceptance of the dominant ideology is best established in childhood, before any awkward questions may be asked. Female acceptance of, even desire for, their role in housework and childcare is established very young. In whose interest is this sex-role organisation? Do employers benefit? Do men? And are women oppressed and exploited by this system? These are questions that will be raised throughout the text. For now, let us briefly assess the evidence that males and females are naturally different and then move on to assess how any differences may be interpreted.

Biological differences between the sexes

Many parents in many cultures express the desire for their first-born to be a son. This may be so, but boy babies are more difficult to get and keep than girls. Although more males are conceived, they are more likely to be miscarried or to die of birth trauma or injuries. They have a greater tendency to congenital malformations and infectious diseases and a higher infant mortality rate. Baby girls tend to be between one to six weeks physiologically more mature at birth and they display fewer 'irritability' symptoms; they cry less and sleep more.

Maturational differences between the sexes

It is well documented that girls mature earlier than boys, and that in many societies women have a longer life expectancy than men. Chapter 3, on education, describes some differences in physical and intellectual skills between boys and girls, but it should be noted here that the differences have probably been greatly exaggerated. In fact, the differences between the sex groups are generally smaller than the differences within each group. It is true that girls learn to speak earlier than boys, and that their greater verbal skills remain throughout childhood. Boys seem to develop visual-spatial superiority to girls. However, it is very difficult to separate maturational differences from differences due to education and training and to the motivation given to children to develop sex-appropriate skills. Reading 1 (p.104) describes this further.

Let us now look at how aspiration and expectation might affect a child's gender identity.

Parental aspiration and expectation

It is likely that the first words any of us heard were a declaration of our sex. 'It's a boy' or 'It's a girl' was our first meaningful label.

Our sex had probably been the subject of much speculation for months. Belotti (1975), cites amusing examples of how some parents use folklore to aid prediction: If the woman is ill-tempered during the pregnancy the baby will be female; if her complexion is rosy a boy is on the way. She noted that all the positive indicators predicted the birth of a son. Aidan McFarland transcribed every word uttered in the delivery room of an obstetrics unit and found an overwhelming preoccupation with the baby's sex, with sexual stereotypes abounding:

> Doctor (trying to deliver a reluctant baby): C'mon junior – must be a girl, only a woman would cause all this trouble!
> Aidan McFarland, *The Psychology of Childbirth*, Fontana, 1977

Whether a baby's sex is a delight or a disappointment probably depends upon where he or she arrives in the sibling hierarchy, Oakley (*Women Confined*, 1980) found that where women do express any sex preference for their first baby, they are twice as likely to choose a boy. Continuing the family line through the male still seems to be valued, and in some societies it can be literally a matter of life or death. Female infanticide – the murder of girl babies – may still be practiced in some societies (see Chapter 5).

That baby boys are often weaker and more demanding than baby girls may explain why they get more attention in the early months. The 'theory of reciprocity' indicates that a baby may shape parental behaviour as much as the other way around. The more vulnerable infant male might experience more encouragement to grow in strength and independence. Moss, Goldberg and Lewis (in *The Psychology of Sex Differences*, 1974), amongst others, have demonstrated that mothers are more likely to handle and fondle their boys, although this pattern changes at around six months when boys experience more encouragement to exploratory behaviour than do girls.

Adults seem to ascribe personality traits very early in the infant's life. Maccoby and Jacklin (1974), who, you will remember, found few gender-specific directives being given to children, nevertheless state that 'Adults respond as if they find boys more interesting and more attention-provoking than girls.' Parents interviewed 24 hours after the birth of their child tended to describe them as 'small and beautiful' or 'strong and vigorous' according to their sex, whereas impartial observers could find no difference at all. A similar study found that adults asked to hold a fully clothed baby and guess its sex, based their decision on whether the infant felt 'soft and fragile' or 'strong'. In fact, the same baby was used throughout the experiment.

It does seem that babies arrive to be greeted with pre-existing, gendered definitions about them. The implications for sex-role socialisation are obvious.

Role learning and role models

Figure 2.1 shows some of the ways children may experience sex-role socialisation, other than by directive.

It is possible that boys' and girls' general socialisation is quite similar for, in Western culture, all children are encouraged to be polite, helpful, honest and achievement motivated. However, sex roles do exist and most children witness significant adults fulfilling them.

There is substantial evidence that children are aware of sex-roles by the age of two. The appropriateness of certain toys,

Fig. 2.1 Ways of learning gender conformity

1 Positive reinforcement – children not necessarily punished for gender-inappropriate behaviour, but subtly rewarded for being 'just like a girl' or 'a big strong boy'

2 Parental expectation – parents pre-conceived ideas about male or female behaviour bring about a self-fulfilling prophecy.

3 Identification and imitation – the behaviour of significant adults and children's heroes and heroines prompt children to take on that behaviour themselves.

4 Peer group pressure – the desire to conform, to be accepted as 'normal' begins early and may increase around adolescence.

games and behaviour also shows class differences, with less rigid stereotyping amongst middle-class children. Hartup and Moore (1963), for example, found girls less reluctant to play or behave like boys than vice versa, and in this respect it might appear that girls enjoy fewer restrictions and greater freedom than boys. However, it could also be argued that even in childhood there exists what Long Laws (1979) describes as 'a vigorous rejection of all things feminine'. 'Tomboys' are regarded indulgently, as 'going through a phase' whereas an effeminate boy will experience greater pressure to conform to his sex-role. Perhaps 'cissy' is the worst epithet a little boy can endure. There is evidence that boys are more actively discouraged from gender-inappropriate behaviour than are girls. Adults are likely to encourage a boy to be 'manly' by, say, discouraging any display of emotion. Boys are quick to pick up on this and apply similar pressure to their peers. Witness the jeers and ridicule suffered by the young classroom offender who is made to 'go and sit with the girls'!

In their longitudinal study of sex-role socialisation, the Newson's found considerable polarisation of behaviour by the age of seven:

It is already noticeable by seven years – and still more by eleven – that the reported preoccupations and hobbies of the two sexes have drawn apart. Indeed, they have polarised so

sharply that a totally biological explanation is tempting, pre-
sumably also involving a maturational hypothesis. We should
keep in mind, however, that cultural factors are frequently
responsible for sharp discontinuities in the way people think
and feel and operate in prescribed social roles, and that sex
roles are not an exception to this just because they also have to
subsume physiological maturational patterns.

> John and Elizabeth Newson, 'Perspectives in Sex-Role
> Stereotyping' in *The Sex Role System*,
> Routledge and Kegan Paul, 1978

Although children born within the last twenty years are less
likely to have parents who fall neatly into the pattern of
housewife–mother and working–father, they are still likely to
find plenty of gendered behaviour on which to model their own.
Through the process of internalisation, children learn to identify
with their own sex and the child who sees only mother responsible for housework develops a taken–for–granted concept of
female activity. Encouragement to join in sex–specific activity is
another critical feature of developing sex–role identity. The
Newson's study (*op.cit.*) found that 72 per cent of mothers and 46
per cent of fathers shared an interest with their 11 year old
daughter, whilst 46 per cent of mothers and 65 per cent of fathers
shared an interest with their son. They also found that certain
household tasks tended to be gender specific.

(It is an interesting point that the Newsons' asked only *mothers*
about the distribution of household chores.)

Figure 2.2 Eleven-year-olds' participation in household duties

Duty	Boys	Girls	Both
		(percentages)	
Washing up	40	63	51
Indoor housework (tidying, vacuum–cleaning, bedmaking etc.)	19	44	32
Miscellaneous dirty/outdoor jobs (gardening, sweeping yard, shoecleaning etc.)	36	8	22
Going on errands	39	21	30

Source: John and Elizabeth Newson, *op.cit.*

The implications of this polarisation of activity are illustrated by Condry and Condry's study (in *The Psychology of Sex Differences,* 1974). They found that children asked to watch a male and female performing the same action on a split screen consistently watched their own sex.

In their attempts to make sense of their world, children often distort and over-generalise but their generalisations are often based on strongly held societal beliefs:

> One little girl looked at the picture of a woman bus driver and said 'Ladies can't drive'. And a child whose mother is a teacher was asked what job her mother had. 'She does dishes' she said. 'Is that all?' we asked. 'Well, she cleans too.'
>
> Programme devised by Women's Action Alliance

We next see how children may be given generous assistance in the formation of such attitudes.

The ideology of children's toys and books

In the sixteenth century Montaigne wrote, 'It should be noted that children at play are not playing about; their games should be seen as their most serious minded activity.'

Educationalists stress the importance of the toys, books, stories and songs that children are offered, for through play children 'rehearse' their adult roles and develop imaginative skills. By two years some children are aware that there exist sex-differentiated ways of playing:

Interviewer:	What do girls do?
Girl:	Make things; make dollie's clothes.
Boy:	I play Incredible Hulk and Superman.
Interviewer:	Do boys play with doll's houses?
Children:	(gasp of surprise) No!
Interviewer:	Why not?
Boy:	'Cos girls do it!

BBC Series *Masculine, Feminine,* 1981

It has been noted already that femininity is considered highly undesirable for a boy. Contempt for feminine activity begins early it seems.

The theory that the differential abilities of boys and girls (small as they are) can be attributed to the different toys they play with is an interesting one. Perhaps the 'people orientation' of girls toys, such as dolls and nurses uniforms, and the 'thing-orientation' of boys toys such as construction sets and toy cars, influence the development of certain skills and interests. What does seem certain is that these toys contribute to gender identity.

But toys are not the only medium of sex-specific messages to children. It is a sad child indeed who is never read a story or shown a picture book, but until very recently, it was difficult to buy children's literature that did not impart stereotypical ideas about men and women:

> Because books for young children explicitly articulate the prevailing cultural values, they are an especially useful indicator of societal norms. . . These books are often read over and over again at a time when children are in the process of developing their sexual identities.
>
> Glynis Loban, *Sexism in Children's Books*, Writers and Readers Publishing Cooperative, 1976

Kathleen McGrath identifies three common features of popular literature:

1 A sequence of recurrent events.
2 Statements of 'what ought to be'; the way a society conceives of itself as a civilised structure.
3 Identification of those forces (human or otherwise) which threaten that civilised structure.

> K. McGrath, *Images of Women in Fiction*, Bowling Green University Popular Press, 1972

This is the formula for most traditional folk and fairy tales. The 'recurrent event' is the maiden in a dilemma and her rescue by a male (Rapunzel, Red Riding Hood, etc). 'What ought to be' is implicit in the female=weak/male=strong theme and in the eventual triumph of good over evil. (The wolf gets beaten by the woodcutter or Cinderella finds her handsome prince.) McGrath's final point, 'the forces that threaten civilised life' are the human or animal villains or the female who creates all the trouble by not following the rules. (What business had Red Riding Hood straying alone in forests, anyway?)

Female characters in such stories fall into two, easily identifiable types. There is the good, beautiful heroine and the wicked witch. Active, powerful characters of the second type are inevitably put in their place by the end of the story. Ann Oakley (1981) argues that 'the myth of feminine evil is a pervasive cultural theme'. Good female characters are usually rewarded by marriage. Male characters in these stories are much more active and take care of themselves; witness how Peter deals with the wolf, for example. Male protagonists are also involved in rescuing damsels from other male predators.

Contemporary children's fiction does little to redress the balance or even accurately represent the changing roles of men and women. An American study (Zaplinski, 1976) analysed books which have won awards for children's fiction, and began with the assumption that if no bias existed, there would be representative samples of male and female characters. That is, in a society where females comprise 52 per cent of the population (in the USA, 51 per cent) that is what the books should represent. The ratios they actually found are as follows:

Males to females in pictures: 11:1
Males to females in titles: 8:3
Males to females in animals
    with clear sex identity: 95:1

One third of the books contained no females at all and where females did appear it was most often in loving, watching and helping roles. Boys were most often depicted performing heroic, exciting feats. In summary, they found three main features:

1 Sex stereotyping – women and men, boys and girls, performing in accordance with rigid and often outdated notions of gender appropriate behaviour.
2 Invisible women – women do not appear at all.
3 Unrealistic images – women portrayed only as wives, mothers, aunties, etc.

> Suzanne M. Czaplinski, 'Sexism in Award Winning Picture Books', in *Sexism in Childrens Books*, Writers and Readers Publishing Cooperative, 1976

Television offers few alternative visions of men and women. Even Wonderwoman managed to look stunning whilst performing her feats of daring in a costume designed to enhance the length of her beautiful legs!

Sex roles and learned helplessness

It does seem then, that children grow up surrounded by images
and examples of sex-appropriate behaviour. The adoption of
some or all of these definitions of womanhood may present girls
with a particular contradiction, for stereotypical femininity is at
variance with other pressures to be achievement oriented and
independent. Although both sexes are encouraged to achieve
personal and academic excellence and liberal parents prompt
their daughters to be as active, assertive and competitive as their
brothers, *all* girls receive signals which indicate that personal
worth and acceptability depends upon their beauty and appeal to
men. Girls who are encouraged to be self-directing individuals
may come to realise that pursuit of that goal might invoke a
welter of disapproval, for it will mean the adoption of some
'masculine' qualities and may mean shedding the 'feminine'
traits of conformity, passivity and dependence. The realisation of
this incongruity in their lives must be daunting for many girls, at
whatever level of consciousness it occurs. That it invariably
becomes a problem during adolescence may explain why so
many girls opt for the path of 'learned helplessness'. This idea is
developed in the next chapter.

3 Education

A central concern of the sociology of education has been underachievement. Why, after one hundred years of free compulsory education, do some groups fail to achieve scholastic success? From research indicating that some groups are educationally disadvantaged have come various policies designed to overcome and compensate for barriers to educational opportunity. For example, over 90 per cent of British children now attend comprehensive schools, thereby alleviating some of the inequities of the tri-partite system of grammar, secondary modern, and technical schools. Educational and Social Priority Areas attempt to compensate for the effects of materially and culturally impoverished environments, and multi-cultural expertise is being developed in areas with large numbers of immigrant children. However, there presently exist no institutionalised policies to help another group of underachievers – girls.

In 1694, Mary Astell claimed:

> Women are from their very infancy debarred those advantages of education the want of which they are afterwards reproached.
>
> Mary Astell, *A Serious Proposal to the Ladies*, London, 1694

Almost 300 years after Astell wrote, no woman is 'debarred' access to education but girls still do not achieve the same success as boys, particularly in the subjects required to gain entry to high-status occupations.

The evidence

Tables 2a–2c (p.89) show differential male and female achievement at secondary and post-secondary levels. It is at this stage of a pupil's career that the polarisation of the sexes becomes most marked. At infant and junior levels there exists some differentiation of interest but, in general, girls score slightly higher on most forms of intellectual test. By the secondary and post–secondary stage the situation has changed (see Figure 3.1).

Fig. 3.1
Synopsis of differential female and male achievement in secondary, further and higher education
1 Girls take and pass more examinations at 16+ but there is already marked sex-differentiation of subject choice.
2 By Advanced (A) level girls are under-represented, particularly in maths, science and technology.
3 There are substantially fewer women in universities and fewer still by postgraduate level; female under-representation in scientific and technological studies extremely marked by now.
4 Women are well represented in further education, particularly in vocational courses for clerical and caring professions. They are less likely than males to receive day release or opportunities for further training from their employers.

As one commentator put it: 'What happens to our most promising students?'. Some research suggests that males and females have different types of intelligence. This argument will be examined next.

Sex differences in intellectual functioning

Meritocratic accounts of the educational system state that those pupils with high intelligence and a capacity for hard work are the ones who succeed. We might wish to challenge that but for now we will assess the evidence that higher levels of male achievement may be due to higher levels of intelligence. Before beginning, it is important to remember three key points:

1 The differences between the sex groups are smaller than the differences within them. That is, groups of men and groups of

women will have a similar spread of measurable intelligence within them.

2 The term *intelligence* is difficult to define. Tests may be designed to measure up to 120 different intellectual functions and, even using the tests, it is impossible to know an individual's potential intelligence in that function. It is, perhaps, safest to say that intelligence tests test what intelligence tests test!

3 As Bowles and Gintis (in *Schooling in Capitalist America* 1976) showed, intelligence tests may predict academic success but they are poor indicators of occupational reward. Variables such as race, sex and social class have greater effect on job chances than intelligence as measured by the means presently available.

Allowing for these problems, it is difficult to be sure of findings which purport to show sex differences in intelligence. One study though, suggested that women score slightly higher on most forms of test: Wechsler's 1939 study led him to suggest that there existed a small but measurable overall superiority of women in levels of general intelligence. However, replication of his tests in 1955 found a slight male superiority on the same criteria. What had changed during those years was the length of schooling experienced by the subjects; by the later tests the men had averaged two years longer in school than the women. Subsequent studies have confirmed that length and quality of education significantly affects intelligence test scores.

However, girls do seem to score more highly on verbal tests and tests of social skills such as anticipating the needs of others. Also responses to non-verbal clues are more developed in girls and women. One study, which monitored the social behaviour of children in six very different cultures found:

In five of the six cultures, girls helped adults and other children more often than did the boys, and in all six groups girls offered psychological support more frequently than did boys. By contrast, the boys, in the majority of cultural settings, more often sought attention from adults and attempted to dominate other children.

Whiting and Whiting, 1975, in Jerome Kagan, *The Growth of the Child*, Harvester Press, 1979

Girls possess greater tactile sensitivity and manual dexterity than boys and they have heightened auditory capacity. However, during late childhood and early adolescence, boys begin to excel in tasks involving mathematical and visual/spatial concepts. It is hardly surprising then that boys choose these areas of study when subject options are made. There is evidence that boys have some measure of innate visual superiority and their sex-role socialisation probably offered them more chance to construct, build and explore than their sisters – all prerequisites to high levels of ability in concepts such as space, volume and measurement.

Given that the medium of all education is language, it would seem reasonable to suggest that girls should be advantaged in every subject. However, what differences there are are subject to modification. For example, although females retain their verbal precocity, males can and indeed do achieve very high levels of verbal ability. In Reading 1 (p.104) McGuinness (1976) argues that girls do not receive the same encouragement to develop cross-sex skills as do boys and that many of the skills in which girls excel are undervalued both in school and in society as a whole. The evidence available at present provides but a small part of the overall pattern of differential achievement. Further, it is necessary to examine not only individual differences but also the different *experiences* of boys and girls within school, and to discover whether educational aims differ for boys and girls.

Education: purpose and function

Most pupils and many educators would see education as a means to 'getting a good job', and indeed Functionalist and Marxist sociologies find a broad measure of agreement about the purpose of education. They believe that schools socialise young people, prepare them for the world of work and act as agents of selection for the occupational hierarchy. In the 1960s, Theodore Schultz coined the term 'Human Capital Theory' to describe the investment made in education which is later realised in wages and status. Although a direct correlation between educational success and occupational reward has been much questioned since then, schools continue to reward some pupils and not others with paper qualifications as a basis for job selection. It is on this issue that Marxist and Functionalist accounts of education differ, for while the latter see schools as neutral agencies rewarding the most able, Marxist theorists describe them as serving the interests of the ruling class and ensuring what Bourdieu calls 'Cultural Reproduction'. ('Cultural Reproduction and Social Reproduction' in Brown, 1973.)

It is tempting to develop this argument with regard to the role of women and argue that if women are to provide a secondary, low-paid labour force within the wage-economy and provide the unpaid social reproduction outside of it, then schools perform a vital function in teaching girls to accept these roles and providing them with the necessary skills such as typing, cookery and so on. Further, schools must perpetuate the ideology that these skills are low-status and therefore low-paid.

Another interpretation is offered by radical feminists who believe that patriarchy contributes to female underachievement:

> Many men can argue genuinely – from their position as men – that there is no prejudice, that there is no discrimination, that women have equal access to their system but choose not to take the right subjects, to obtain the necessary qualifications, to gain the right experience. If men perceive their standards, based on their experience, as the *only* standard (and the only human experience) then it is reasonable for them to argue that women simply do not 'measure up' in their terms.
>
> Dale Spender, *Invisible Women*, Writers and
> Readers Publishing Cooperative, 1982

Other social theorists have argued that one function of the school is that of persuading certain groups that they have 'failed' and that failure is their own fault; they have not acquired the skills and knowledge considered valuable in education and society. The sociology of knowledge goes beyond such taken-for-granted assumptions about what is deemed to be worthwhile knowledge to examine how knowledge and the value attached to it are generated:

> Are we reluctant to accept that academic curricula and the forms of assessment associated with them are sociological inventions to be explained like men's other inventions, mechanical and sociological?
>
> Michael Young, *Knowledge and Control*,
> Collier Macmillan, 1971

The social construction of knowledge has many implications for an analysis of women's educational experience.

The hidden curriculum

Curriculum and textbooks: style and content

One day a young captain Jonathan
he was eighteen at the time,
Captured a pelican
On an island in the Far East
In the morning,
This pelican
of Jonathan's
Laid a white egg
and out of it came
A pelican
Astonishingly like the first.
And this second pelican
laid in its turn
A white egg,
From which came inevitably
Another
who did the same again.
This sort of thing can go on
A very long time,
if you don't make an omelette.

Robert Desnos, *'Chantefleurs, Chantefables'*

This poem prefaced a set of readings called *Knowledge and Control*, which examined the social construction of knowledge and assessed the means by which some forms of knowledge and not others come to be defined and considered of high status. The book's editor, Michael Young, believed, 'Academic curricula in this country involve assumptions that some kinds and areas of knowledge are much more 'worthwhile' than others.' How does this happen?

According to Marx, 'the ideas of the ruling class are in every epoch the ruling ideas'. The response of some working-class children to these 'ruling–class ideas' is very well researched.

Hargreaves, and later P. Willis (*Learning to Labour*, 1978), de-scribed how aggressive, anti-school subcultures may develop among working–class boys who are rejected by school and who themselves reject the school's ideology.

Similarly, the linguistic form in which knowledge is transmit-ted can cause problems for children. It is easy to develop this idea with regard to women students who, glancing through their books or listening to their teacher may be led to believe that women barely exist! Spender coined the term 'Invisible Women' to describe this phenomena.

Use of the term 'man' to mean all humanity or of the pronoun 'he' to signify a person of either sex, constitutes what Wendy Martyna ('Beyond the 'He/Man' Approach; the case for Non-sexist Language' in *The Woman Question*, 1982) describes as 'a major roadblock on the path toward a language that speaks clearly and fairly of both sexes'. Objections to the use of the generic 'man' may seem trivial, but language shapes thought and marks boundaries in a culture. Sapir in *Language, Culture and Personality* (1949) claims that 'All in all, it is not too much to say that one of the really important functions of language is to be constantly declaring to society the psychological place of all its members.' You may wish to examine your own texts for women's invisibility in language and could start with an example from a recent sociology textbook which opens its chapter on stratification:

> *Men* have long dreamed of an egalitarian society, a society in which all members are equal. In such a society *men* will no longer be ranked in terms of prestige. . . *Men* will be equal in the sight of God and in the eyes of their fellow *men*.'
>
> M. Haralambos, *Sociology: themes and perspectives*,
> UTP, 1980 [my emphasis]

But women are not only ignored linguistically, they are fre-quently ignored or misrepresented in curriculum content also. Table 1 (p.88) shows the unrepresentative portrayal of women characters in children's reading schemes. There may be very little change by the time the student reaches A-level standard (see Figure 3.2):

Marion Scott analysed the content of textbooks used in secon-dary schools and found that where women were mentioned at all, it was often very stereotypically (see Figure 3.3).

Figure 3.2 Sex of authors of prescribed A-level texts in English literature, 1977–1978

Examining Board	Women writers	Men writers
London University	1	26
AEB	0	15
Metropolitan Examining Board	1	10
Total	2	51

Source: Anna Walters in *Learning to Lose*, Women's Press, 1980

A further stumbling block is the school timetable. Many timetables are organised so that 'girls' subjects and 'boys' subjects are offered only as alternatives. It simply may not be possible to take both domestic science and woodwork. The London Institute of Education Curriculum Studies Department defines curriculum as 'a selection from the culture of society'. It has been argued that women students cannot develop a positive image of their sex whilst 'the selection from the culture' offers them so few positive and encouraging images of women.

Pupil-teacher interaction and teachers' expectations

So far educational experience has been described as if teachers and pupils are passive subjects with little or no control over what happens in the classroom. However, interactionist approaches to education show how students and teachers are in a continuous process of negotiating meanings, and that both bring to the classroom some 'taken for granted' assumptions about each other.

A teacher's ability to make decisions about, or 'label' a student has been found to have far-reaching effects on the behaviour and achievement of pupils. This phenomenon has become known as the 'self-fulfilling prophecy'. A teacher's 'gendered expectations' may well affect a girl's education chances. Research funded by the Equal Opportunities Commission on *Girl Friendly Schooling* (1984), analysed the views of 850 teachers and found that although the majority believed in the *policy* of equal opportunities, very few were committed to any sort of *practice* to ensure equality. They also found frequent examples of teachers who believed a boy's education to be more important than a girl's. A

Fig. 3.3 Typical textbook content in three subjects

Mathematics
The world of maths is male and this is reinforced in several books by the number of questions which revolve around men and boys doing things which are susceptible to mathematical calculation. . . occasional gestures towards the girls being included in maths are made, typically via a girl sipping tea or standing decoratively posed in a mini-skirt in a 'phone booth. . .

Chemistry and physics
The male predominates in the pictures, examples and questions. . . a focus on the history of science dealing with the main discoverers who all seem to be men. . .

History
Typical was a view of the past which left women invisible. A book on the First World War made no mention of women's contribution to the war effort at home or abroad. A book on Britain since 1700 ignored the nineteenth century feminists and the birth control movement. Books on political and economic history were almost exclusively about men. . . the reader could be forgiven for reaching the conclusion that there have been no social changes which have involved/affected women. . .

Marion Scott, 'Teach Her a Lesson: sexist curriculum in patriarchal education' in *Learning to Lose*, Women's Press, 1980

similar study, also published in 1984, showed how over 40 per cent of teachers did not believe a girl's career to be as important as a boy's.

It is likely that such beliefs will be translated into classroom practice. Indeed, Kathy Clarricotes (1978) found that teachers nearly always assessed boys as brighter, even when girls were scoring higher grades. Dale Spender's (1981) classroom observations revealed that teachers spend up to two-thirds of their time on the boys in the class and were far more likely to remember the names of males students.

Even when informed of their extra attention to boys, teachers find it a difficult pattern to correct, possibly because boys in class are more likely to be demanding, attention seeking and assertive. Teachers describe their girls as 'nice' or 'neat' emphasising their passivity and conformity, as compared to the 'naughty' behaviour of some boys. Gender non-conformity may meet with as much ridicule from staff as from other students:

> The (male) teacher asked me if I would like to be a Muslim. I said 'no' and he asked why. Apart from the fact that I am an atheist. . . I said that I did not agree with purdah and male chauvinism. He said, 'Are you one of those women's libbers then, girl?' I said yes, to which he replied, 'Oh mah gawd, we've got a right one 'ere.' I thought I must be some sort of crank because everyone, including the other girls, laughed.
>
> 14-year-old schoolgirl, in *Spare Rib*, no. 75, October 1978

Teachers frequently use gender as an organising principle in the classroom, especially with younger pupils. They can thereby highlight sex divisions or set boys and girls in competition with each other. Sex stereotyped assumptions about pupils may be vocalised:

> Why, Maureen, you've had your hair cut, you look quite a young lady. Such a helpful child she always offers to put the toys away. A little boisterous for a girl but she's quieting down. . . Emma, little girls don't fight like that. . . Alex could you be very grown up and take this over to the junior school to Mr Jones?. . . he's a real little boy, you know, quite a tearaway at times.
>
> Primary teachers quoted in Eileen Byrne,
> *Women and Education*, Tavistock, 1978

Older, female students may encounter sexual innuendo, teasing and comments about body or appearance and male teachers may draw attention to a girl pupil's sexuality:

> Classroom harassment runs through the whole familiar spectrum, from the uncomfortable feeling you are being eyed up, through suggestive remarks, jokes, and groping to 'serious' propositions of sex. Tutors do not ignore the personal and

intellectual qualities of their female students but these can come second to burning questions like 'Is the attractive?' 'Will she, won't she?' No encounter or assessment remains free from this cattle-market mentality.

Deborah Cameron, 'Sex with your tutor? It's his fringe benefit', *Spare Rib*, no. 99, November 1980

In Reading 2, p.105, there is an extract from Michelle Stanworth's latest research into teachers' different gender expectations.

Organisation and staffing

Another aspect of a schools 'hidden curriculum' which militates against the full development of female potential is the school's internal organisation and staffing patterns. Although women teachers are in the majority in junior schools they cluster on the lowest pay-scales. The longer a student stays in full-time education the more marked the pattern of female subordination becomes and the more males she will encounter in positions of power and authority.

The next section shows how pupils 'act out' their internalisation of the sex-role.

Pupil aspiration and motivation

Adolescent girls may discover that the demands of academic excellence conflict with the demands of 'femininity.' Matima Horner (1976) described *The Motive to Avoid Success* as a possible resolution to this dilemma; young women may decide not to compete with their male peers but work to seek their approval instead. Male students do not experience this conflict, for ambition, drive and dedication are thoroughly acceptable male qualities. Komarovsky's research in 1946 showed that women students often 'play down' or belittle their own achievements when in the presence of male colleagues or boyfriends. Thirty years later, Sue Sharpe found how girls were perfectly well aware that boys did not like girls who were 'too clever'.

Similar and related findings describe how students attribute their success. A repeated result is that girls attribute their success to 'luck' or an easy exam, whilst boys have more confidence in their own ability and hard work. Further, aspiration and motivation levels are critically associated with class.

Sex and class

Women's education is not a simple issue of all girls receiving the same education or reaching the same levels of attainment. Some women do succeed in the educational system, some even in the 'male' spheres of maths and electronics. However, these women are exceptional and more likely to have middle-class backgrounds. Schools may expect different standards of middle-class and working-class girls:

> One of the central features of the school is to prepare pupils for the position they will occupy in the labour force. This process is obviously not simply a matter of feeding pupils automatically into some slot in the labour market. . . for our purposes here, it is enough to point to the fact that in this process working-class girls are separated out from their middle-class counterparts. So although both may be the targets of sexist practices in the school, there are also differences in the way these oppressive factors operate and in the way they are responded to. To put it crudely, middle-class girls are directed to different kinds of jobs than working-class girls although both may also be, indeed are, pushed in the direction of the home. Wolpe (1976) describes schooling for working-class girls as an attempt to produce 'an adaptable, pliable and docile labour source with only marginal skills.'
>
> Angela McRobbie, 'Working-class girls and the culture of femininity', in *Women Take Issue*, Hutchinson, 1978

In her study, McRobbie found that working-class girls often rejected the school's ideology of femininity which involved passivity and quiet obedience and replaced it with an aggressively sexual one, sometimes disrupting the class with talk of boy-friends, make-up and so on. When asked how they spent their time in the maths lesson, two girls replied:

> Sue: 'Carve names on me desk, anything that comes into me head – boy's names. Woody, Eric, Les – then when I've done that I start writing on me plimsoles.'

Karen: 'Comb me hair under the lid of the desk, put on make-up, look in me mirror.'

Angela McRobbie, *op.cit.*

Working-class girls, then, may suffer the dual bind of conflicting home-school values coupled with the pressures to achieve feminine success through beauty and making relationships. Their response may be a rejection of school, rejection of passivity and compliance and the adoption of an alternative definition of themselves as desirable females and potential wives and mothers. Both these alternative aspirations severely limit their chances of educational success and potential careers. They are, believes McRobbie, 'both saved and locked within the culture of femininity'. Some writers believe the 'culture of masculinity' to be no less of a problem.

The culture of masculinity

A masculine ideal which allows competition and aggressive individualism may take its toll. The alternative status sought by boys who fail in the system may result in an aggressively 'macho' stance, dangerous to themselves and to others. Madeline Arnot describes this in Reading 3 (p.107)

Spender (*Invisible Women*, 1982) argued that the reason textbooks and teachers concentrate on topics that will interest boys is because classroom control is much harder when *boys* are disaffected and bored. Research by Zimmerman and West in *Language and Sex, Difference and Dominance* (1975), shows that in *all* social situations males talk more, are more likely to control the direction of discussion and to interrupt more frequently than females. Even quite young boys have learned these techniques of control and will use them, not only on their peers but frequently on their female teachers also. Let us now look at how some educators are attempting to overcome these difficulties.

The response

Some schools have formulated policies to help overcome 'gendered' educational practice. They may, for example, ensure that timetables are not organised in a way that would make it

impossible to follow, say needlework *and* woodwork and have
introduced assertiveness training for girls and boys in single sex
groups. They invite men and women following 'opposite sex'
occupations to come and talk to students about their jobs. Some
offer half-term courses on sex-role stereotyping and special
resources may be developed to present more positive images of
women. Curriculum materials can be monitored for sexism and
women's achievements and contributions included in course
content.

However, such changes are slow to evolve and work of this
kind is usually done on an ad hoc basis, dependent upon the
goodwill and commitment of one or two teachers within a
school. The reluctance of some teachers and administrators to
implement such policy is probably due in part to the belief that
no discrimination exists and that equal opportunities *are* provided.

There are suggestions that co-educational schooling is partly
responsible for female under-achievement:

> In a society whose very structure, practices and beliefs are
> heavily marked by socially constructed gender divisions, the
> sexes do not stand equal on admission to secondary school,
> and offering both girls and boys the *same* opportunities and
> facilities cannot lead to equality of opportunity, still less
> equality of outcome.
>
> Rosemary Deem, *Co-Education Reconsidered*,
> Open University Press, 1984

The arguments are complex but rest on the belief that girls
perform better when not having to compete with boys, and that
women teachers in the sciences and maths as well as holding
posts of responsibility in the school, provide good role models
for young women. The National Foundation for Educational
Research study of 1964 and the 1980 Survey of Mathematical
Development both found better maths results from girls in
single-sex schools. However, it is difficult to generalise from
these results as most single-sex schools are remaining grammar
schools and the higher test scores could be due to higher ability.
One secondary modern school, Stamford High School, was
concerned about girls' maths scores and established one all-girls
first-year maths set, monitored their results across two years and
compared them with the scores of boys and girls in mixed sets.

Figure 3.4 shows how the girls in the single-sex set were, after two years, scoring more highly than their female peers in the mixed set.

Figure 3.4 Test scores in maths – mixed and single-sex sets at Stamford High School

	October 1978	November 1979	February 1980	June 1980
All girls set	58.9	55.1	54.7	51.6
Girls in equivalent mixed set	58.0	50.0	43.9	38.1
Boys in equivalent mixed set	59.0	59.0	56.4	49.3

Source: Stuart Smith in *Co-Education Reconsidered* Rosemary Deem (ed.), Open University Press, 1984

We must however, be cautious about generalising from such findings and, indeed there is still a great deal to be known about the reasons for female underachievement. Sex, as a variable of educational achievement, has never had the academic or political 'pull' that class and race have had. The situation may be changing now but it seems unlikely that just establishing single-sex groups will reverse present trends unless other positive steps are also taken. 'Girl friendly schooling' would involve in-service training for teachers, awareness programmes for pupils and close scrutiny of curriculum content in order to eliminate bias. At present, only a few schools or eduction authorities have declared their commitment to such policies.

4 Marriage and domestic labour

The cosy image of the working husband, economically inactive wife and dependent children so beloved of the advertisers, in fact accounts for only 15 per cent of families. Housewifery, however, is still a predominantly female occupation and one which social theorists have ignored until very recently. In 1981, 72 per cent of men and 79 per cent of women over the age of sixteen were, or had been, married. However, Jessie Bernard (*The Future of Marriage*, 1976) points out that marriage is not experienced in the same way for both partners and that 'her' marriage may be considerably less satisfactory than 'his'. This may explain why seven out of ten divorces are filed by women.

Following divorce, separation or the death of a spouse, men are likely to remarry more quickly than women. Perhaps this is a result of a culture which allows men to do the 'chasing' whilst women must wait to be asked, but it may also be attributed to a society which allows men expression of their emotions only within a relationship with a woman:

> A man may feel that he must woo a woman with his masculinity. When he first meets a woman he feels under some pressure to perform with confidence and assertiveness. He 'knows' that this is what women are supposed to be attracted to and he wants to be successful in his love affairs. But at the same time, men are eager to have a woman with whom they can share another part of themselves. It may only be with a woman that a man's emotional vulnerability emerges. It is taboo for men to expose that aspect of their personalities to each other for it signifies emotionality and femininity.
>
> Luise Eichenbaum and Susie Orbach,
> *What Do Women Want?*, Fontana, 1984

Perhaps the freedom to express emotion and vulnerability contributes to the improvement in men's physical, emotional and mental health with marriage. Women's health, however, does not benefit from marriage. Table 4 (p.94) shows the evidence for Bernard's claim that marriage, 'quite literally makes women sick'. The section on 'Housework as work' may offer some explanation of this.

In 1963, Betty Friedan identified 'the problem without a name':

> Each suburban housewife stuggled with it alone. As she made the beds, shopped for groceries, matched slip cover material, ate peanut butter sandwiches with her children, chauffeured Cub Scouts and Brownies, lay beside her husband at night, she was afraid to ask even of herself the silent question 'Is this all?'
>
> Betty Friedan, *The Feminine Mystique*, Penguin, 1963

This work exposed for the first time the fact that many women did not find the fulfilment they hoped for in marriage. Friedan suggested that idealised and highly unrealistic images of romantic love lead to disillusion, and that her study was a 'damning indictment' of the 'feminine mystique'.

Since the publication of Friedan's work there have been many other studies of family life in Britain and America, some of which suggest that stereotypical sex-role segregation within marriage is being eroded. Willmott and Young's (1975) controversial study of 'the symmetrical family' suggested that the family is evolving into a stage where men may be more home-centred and women more likely to have careers. They claim a 'symmetry' to conjugal role relationships which other studies have failed to support.

Time-budget studies in Britain and America quite clearly dispel the myth of the egalitarian household whilst the 1985 survey, *Social Trends*, shows how even male manual workers enjoy around six hours per week more leisure time than their wives (see also Table 5, p.95, and Reading 7, p.111). But surely domestic technology has reduced the tedium and drudgery of housework? It seems not, for as Oakley has explained, rising expectations of domestic comfort and cuisine have taken up any extra time domestic technology provides. In addition, increasing numbers of wives and mothers taking paid work may find that they now face a double load.

Couples who wish to break free of stereotypical role relationships and share domestic work and childcare while both partners follow a career, face many problems. These are outlined in Figure 4.1 and in Reading 7 (p.111). The rest of this chapter

Fig. 4.1 Egalitarian marriage: changes and obstacles
This table outlines some of the changes required in order
to effect a redistribution of work and domestic role allocation. It shows the changes necessary and the obstacles to
those changes. There is a high degree of overlap; for
example, internalisation of sex role obviously affects the
degree to which the other three can be successful. In
addition, 1, 2 and 3 all require radical policy changes not
only from government but also from industry and com-
merce.

Changes required	*Obstacles to be overcome*
1 Re-allocation of responsibility for childcare	Lack of adequate childcare facilities; inflexibility of present school hours and holidays.
2 Reorganisation of productive work	Inflexibility of working hours; insufficient job-sharing schemes; no paternity leave.
3 Reorganisation of family life	Decision about role re-allocation; decisions about coping with emergency, such as the sickness of children. Two partners now expected to 'juggle' conflicting demands of home and career.
4 Internalisation of sex role	Difficulties of reviewing highly developed, internalised notions of masculinity and femininity. For example, mothers may experience guilt, fathers may experience resentment. Partners may experience jealousy and competition especially if both are highly motivated and committed to a demanding career; pressure from others to conform.

Source: adapted from: Fran Pepitone Rockwell, *Dual Career
Couples*, Sage Publications, 1980

will examine the role of housewife, and starts with some of the explanations which have been offered as to why cooking, cleaning and childcare are seen to be 'women's work'.

Why housewives?

Biology is destiny

This is a very popular idea which supposes that the sexes' anatomical differences predispose them to different types of activity. For example, 'the maternal instinct' is ill-defined but supposed to be common among women. Oakley (*Becoming a Mother*, 1976) found that 61 per cent of women believed in it but that only 36 per cent found they had it when confronted with their own babies. Other theories presuppose a link between biological and social activity.

Tiger and Fox (*The Imperial Animal*, 1972) believe that men are 'naturally' assertive and strong and that women are 'naturally' passive, dependent and weak. G. Murdock (*Social Structure*, 1949) studied 224 societies and deduced that the sexual division of labour must be a product of biology which renders women weak and bound to home-based activity. Males can perform the strenuous tasks because of their greater physical prowess. Murdock's own evidence proves him wrong (Table 10 p.100), for there are few societies where tasks are performed exclusively by men and it is difficult to deduce how 'water-carrying' and 'burden-bearing' are activities requiring little strength – both these are primarily female activities, according to Murdock's data. The appeal of the above theories is their simplicity but they must be described as pre-sociological for the following reasons:

1 They attempt to explain culture through biology and fail to address cultural variations. Not all societies regard women as 'weak' and only industrial societies expect pregnant and nursing mothers to withdraw from economic activity (see also Reading 6, p.111).
2 They fail to address the problems of the relative values of sex-differentiated activity. For example, physical strength is not the criteria by which pay, status and prestige is awarded in Western culture.

3 They fail to explain why men's work receives pay, status, paid holidays, overtime rates, limited working hours, union protection and health insurance while women's domestic work does not.

For these reasons it is necessary to move beyond such biological determinism to assess the ways in which men and women are also *socially constructed*. For example, functionalist theory describes how biological differences may provide the basis of social differences.

Functionalism: Parsons and the 'expressive role'

In 1956 Parsons, with Bales, published 'Family, Socialisation and Interaction Process', in which he described the two roles within a marriage as *instrumental* or *expressive* (see Fig 4.2). Men's roles were seen as *instrumental*: 'Externally the husband had primary adaptive responsibilities relative to the outside situation.' Women's roles were seen as *expressive*, and: 'concern the internal affairs of the system and the maintenance of integrative relations between the members.' Thus, men behave in a purposeful, rational manner to support the family whilst women provide love, security and emotional support for family members. He did note the expressive functions of husbands and fathers but his polarisation of two types of activity has remained a constant theme throughout the literature on family life.

Parson's theory was based upon laboratory experiments conducted by Bales in 1950. In these experiments groups of males were given a task to complete in a co-operative venture. It was found that within groups a task leader emerged who controlled and directed activity and another male emerged who offered social and emotional support as the task progressed. We might speculate that laboratory experiments with groups of males provide a rather poor methodological base upon which to posit a theory about family roles. However, let us see how Parson's theory relates to the work of women in the home.

Margrit Eichler (*The Double Standard: a feminist critique of feminist social science*, 1980) takes Parsons to task about his misconceptions about 'expressive activity'. She describes his interpretation as androcentric, meaning that it is essentially a male point of view. She says that men interpret the housewife role in this way because they are rarely around when it is being performed. This

Fig. 4.2 **Instrumental and expressive roles in marriage**
This table takes the four features that Parsons identified as
characteristics of instrumental activity and shows how
women's so called expressive role involves a great deal of
instrumental activity.

1 *Instrumental activity involves a consumer of the product*
Husband: Public is consumer of product or service and
employer the beneficiary of surplus value.
Wife: Family is consumer of product and beneficiary
of surplus value.

2 *Instrumental activity involves remuneration*
Husband Paid out of own or employer's profit.
Wife: No remuneration unless work is performed out-
side marriage, e.g. cook, cleaner.

3 *Instrumental activity requires access to facilities provided by others*
Husband: Facilities and tools provided in office or factory.
Wife: Facilities provided by gas, water, electricity
companies, agriculture, retail trades.

4 *Instrumental activity requires co-operation and collaboration with
others*
Husband: Co-operates and collaborates with employers,
trade unions and colleagues.
Wife: Co-operates and collaborates with doctors, social workers, teachers, tradespeople.

Or, as one commentator said, 'There's nothing expressive
about taking out the garbage'!

Source: Adapted from Eichler, *op.cit.*

raises the issue of male bias in the social sciences and the
implications for social theory; if housework is not considered
'real' work, not considered worthy of study, it is hardly surprising if theories about it, and its relationship to other areas of
social life are somewhat distorted. Nor does Parson's theory of
complementary but dissimilar roles confront the issue of the
relative *value* attached to each sphere of activity. The next section
offers some analysis of this.

Domestic labour under capitalism

Marxist theorists have attributed the domestic labour of women to the needs of capitalism. Whilst not denying patriarchy (male power and control) in feudal society, they explain how industrialisation moved production from home to factory and contributed to the removal of women from paid work. Thus, men perform productive work which makes surplus value for capital and women perform the tasks of 'social reproduction' as they cook, clean and generally care for the labour force. Capital does not have to bear the cost of this labour as individual husbands cover the expenses from their wage. Women's work has no surplus value as the fruits of her labour never reach the commodity market. Her work enables a capitalist economy to function by providing, free of charge, goods and services which would otherwise have to be paid for:

> The work of the housewife though it has the same material or service effect as that of a chambermaid, restaurant worker, cleaner or laundry worker is outside the purview of capital.
>
> Harry Braverman, *Labour and Monopoly Capital*,
> Monthly Review Press, 1974

The work of the housewife is also largely 'outside the purview' of Braverman's book for it warrants only one mention in a work which claims to analyse 'the degradation of work in the 20th century'. However, he does explain how women's domestic work is labour which, if performed anywhere other than within marriage, would have to be paid for.

Other Marxist analysis describes how domestic labour upholds the economy and how the family provides a market for the ever increasing products of capitalism. Sue Sharpe suggests (in *New Edinburgh Review*, Summer 1972) that the nuclear family, and role of women within it, performs two key functions for capitalism. Firstly, women service and maintain the labour force and secondly, they provide a market for more and more consumer durables. Thus, women's work in the home supports and stimulates the economy. Rowbotham describes how this also entails physical separation of the two spheres of activity:

> Separation of production for use and production for exchange, the physical distance between the place of consumption and the place of production and the social division of

labour between men and women means that the commodity system is as dependent on women's work in the home as on the exploitation of labour outside.

Sheila Rowbotham, *Women, Resistance and Revolution*, London, Allen Lane, 1972

Although these explanations of women's domestic labour offer some understanding of the social construction of the role, they are, nevertheless, open to the charge of economic reductionism; that is, both Marxist and functionalist theory describe economic features of social life as if they had a force over and above the individuals who comprise society. Neither analysis satsifactorily addresses the power relationships that exist between individual men and women in both capitalist and non-capitalist societies. The next section confronts this problem and suggests ways in which male supremacy continues to flourish within marital relationships and indicates how both individual men and capitalism benefit from women's unpaid work.

The housewife role as a remnant of pre-capitalist patriarchy

It may not be possible to analyse domestic labour in terms of a capitalist economic relationship for it is far from proven that women's domestic labour is functional to capitalism (see also Chapters 5 and 7). For example, Marxist theory describes the tendency to 'capital accumulation', which means that capital eventually gains control of all forms of labour. If this is so, why isn't domestic labour and childcare now organised in a way which makes a direct profit for capital? Is the marriage contract, and the duties and obligations that come with it, really a simple economic relationship? The ways in which individual men benefit from this type of domestic organisation has been conspicuously absent from the analysis until recently. Perhaps the reason that Marxist and other analyses have ignored patriarchy as a feature of this organisation is that most of the theorists were men, to whom patriarchy is a 'non-problem'?

Patriarchy is a feature of most societies (see Chapter 6) and in particular, was a feature of feudal society before industrialisation. The adjustment and adaptation of patriarchy to 'fit' capitalism may now form what Heidi Hartmann (1976) calls 'the two interlocking systems of patriarchy and capitalism' (see also p.56).

Whatever their own relationship to the means of production, all married men benefit from their wives' unpaid labour and her economic dependence on him ensures that the situation remains unchanged. In Reading 4 p.108 Eichler describes some of the ways in which a wife's total dependency on her husband resembles a serf's dependency on a lord. A similar phenomenon becomes clear when we consider the market value of a woman's domestic work. Despite the cost of keeping a wife, a man increases the real value of his wage when his wife performs all his domestic services, provides constant sexual access and transforms raw materials into goods (as in cooking or sewing). Such a range of services would probably be beyond the means of most men if they were not to profit from their wives' labour, and instead had to pay for them (directly or indirectly) at the market rate. Seen in this way, all men who benefit from women's unpaid labour can be seen as 'mini–capitalists' for they benefit from the work more than the labourer herself. The exact nature of this labour is discussed next.

Housework as work

Until quite recently sociological interest in women has focused upon two areas of their lives: on (supposedly) changing conjugal roles and on women's increasing participation in waged work. Women's lives have been of interest to social and economic theorists only insofar as they affect or resemble men's.

Students are taught that 'the industrial revolution separated work and home' and that 'women are returning to work' – both pieces of sociological folklore reflecting and reinforcing the notion that women's domestic work is not 'real work'. Judith Long Laws (1979) believes that 'The scholarly literature tends to neglect a whole range of phenomena that figures in women's experience. The gap is greatest in areas where male scholars have least experience.' But it may be little wonder that industrial sociology has ignored domestic labour for no other job presents such problems for analysts. No matter what the social class of the woman the work remains essentially the same. It is extremely difficult to define the working hours of an occupation which is also a way of life. Is the woman who does mending whilst watching TV working or relaxing? Is the woman who sleeps in the same house as her children ever off duty? Stanley Parker acknowledged some of these problems:

> The life of the housewife is like that of the prisoner, it tends to be restricted at both ends of the constraint-freedom scale. . . There is for her no real difference between work and work-obligations and the responsibility of the household, particularly if she is a mother, must often restrict the range of her leisure activities, even though her free time may be greater than that of her working sister.
>
> Stanley Parker, *The Sociology of Industry*,
> George Allen and Unwin, 1972

Sue McKintosh takes Parker to task over his assertion that housewives have much free time:

> To equate being at home with having 'free time' is a thoroughly male assumption, and it is true for most men. For all women, employed or not, being at home is definitely not an experience involving much leisure.
>
> Sue McKintosh *et al.* in *Leisure and Social Control*,
> Brighton Polytechnic, 1981

Ann Oakley's 1974 study of housework (*The Sociology of Housework*) attempted to overcome what she called 'the sociological neglect of housework'. Using Goldthorpe's study of the pressures on 'affluent workers' (1969), Oakley showed how domestic labour brings greater monotony, fragmentation of task and pressure from working at speed than either factory or assembly line work. She also found loneliness to be a critical feature of the housewife's work role. A more detailed summary of her findings is in Reading 5 p.109.

It is hardly surprising, therefore, that housebound women are more prone to physical and emotional/mental illnesses than working women or men (see Table 4 p.94). Working-class women suffer more than do middle-class women but even so, work by Brown and Harris (*Social Origins of Depression*, 1978) showed how only 50 per cent of working-class women with depressive illnesses seek or receive treatment. Neither is the home a particularly safe place to be. Many accidents take place in the home and one quarter of all reported crimes of violence is wife abuse. In 1975, the Parliamentary Select Committee on Violence in Marriage estimated that one in every hundred women may experience physical abuse from her husband. One explanation of why women continue to be housewives is provided by an analysis of the ideology which surrounds the role.

The ideology of femininity

We have noted already the enormous difficulties faced by couples who wish to find alternative ways of organising their family and domestic life. Aside from these problems, women and men who wish to reject stereotypical sex-roles must also reject their internalisation of those roles; our sense of self is intricately interwoven with notions of masculinity and femininity. Images of being a wife and mother are part of women's subjectivity. They are the only occupations into which workers are socialised from birth and the only occupations so bound with notions of love and duty, and with romantic illusions about women's reproductive functions. Despite increasing tolerance of sexual activity outside marriage, women's sexuality is still strongly tied to marriage, and social disapproval still meets women who are unashamedly sexually active or who have children outside marriage. Given the strength of the ideology, the role of women within marriage is highly resistant to change.

Throughout this chapter we have raised the issues of the difficulties of analysing domestic labour by existing social theory and of the ways in which social scientists have systematically ignored and/or distorted this important aspect of women's lives. In particular, women pose a problem for theorising about the definition and measurement of social class. It is an area that is beginning to figure prominently in sociology; a brief introduction to the debate is offered here, and in the next chapter.

Housewives: stratification theory and status

According to current social theory, occupation is the key variable in determining an individual's social class. Marx, for example, defined a person's social class by their relationship to the means of production whilst the Registrar General's Scale categorises the occupations found in industrial society into five social classes. Women's unpaid domestic work is omitted from both models, indeed, they are quite untenable for assessing women's class position. For example, the Marxist definition won't work because housewives are even further removed from the means of production, a situation which underlines their dependence on the male and puts them outside class analysis. Neither does housework appear in the RG's scale, comprised, as it is, of only paid work.

Housework is work performed by all women, suggesting that they are all one class. If this is so it is a singularly ill-defined class for it has its reality only in relation to another individual – the husband. Also, where do we place women who also have a paid occupation?

After marriage women are assumed to occupy the same class position as their husbands. Some theorists acknowledge the problem of assessing the class position of families where the woman's work is of a higher social status than the man's. However, the problem is considered only in so far as it calls into question the status of the *family*, not of the individual woman or man. Similarly ignored is a woman's self-assigned status; a study in the USA showed that a substantial number of women believed themselves to be in a different social class from their husbands. Even by more objective criteria, many women are in a different social class than their husbands when wives' occupation before marriage is taken into account. Social theory also suggests that marriage is a possible avenue of social mobility for women although how it can do this whilst simultaneously robbing them of their own social class is difficult to comprehend.

We seem to have arrived at a position where class-based analysis of women is possible only if they are not housewives. Perhaps these confusions arise because sociology has taken *the family* as its unit of analysis? Implicit in such an approach is the belief that women's domestic work is not *real* work, which brings us to the problem of what is considered *work* in social and economic analysis. One author of a current textbook described this tradition thus:

> In official surveys married women and dependent children are allocated to the class of their husband and father. The majority of women *are not in full time work* . . . to a considerable extent therefore, class categorisation by male occupation reflects a family-based social system. There are those who feel that this system of classification illustrates and underlines the inferior

position of women in British society.

M. O'Donnell, *A New Introduction to Sociology*,
Harrap, 1981 [my emphasis]

O'Donnell is making two assumptions: the first is that house-wives' work is not real work, and the second is that the social system is 'family based'. It might be asked, whether 'class categorisation by male occupation' does not rather reflect a 'family based' sociology. Margrit Eichler (1980) suggests that 'it is only when we take the individual rather than the family as the unit of analysis that we can start critically to examine the appropriateness of various stratification theories for women's place in society.'

Married women are omitted from stratification models and excluded from stratification theory because of the way the models are constructed; class analysis is premised on a particular type of economic relationship (employer/employee) whereas women's economic dependence on men is another type of economic relationship altogether. Female dependency cuts across male classes and present theory is unable to incorporate this fact. The anomalies are by-passed by 'lumping' women into the same class position as their husbands – a 'solution' which is intellectually dishonest if not downright cavalier. The marriage relationship is unlike any other in capitalist economies and the unique, and hitherto unexplored, nature of that relationship puts it beyond any attempt to use presently available means of assessment. The problem is, as yet, unresolved but it seems inevitable that future work in this field will radically affect not only class analysis of women but of men too.

Similar, and related questions regarding occupational stratification are introduced on p.56–60.

5 Paid work

The last chapter discussed how women's domestic role may be functional to the present economic system. This theme will be taken up again in the final chapter. Now, we investigate women's participation in waged work; that is, women's participation in the production and exchange of goods and services involving the performance of tasks which are paid for by an employer. The first part of this chapter will look at the current situation of women's employment and the second part will assess the various theories which attempt to explain the situation of women workers.

Liberation or running on the spot?

Women now comprise 40 per cent of the labour force; one third of this figure has entered paid employment since the Second World War. If, as Marx and Engels believed, paid work represents a means to female liberation then there has indeed been a major shift in the relative position of women and men in the last forty years. However, such claims should be regarded with caution. Certainly, increasing numbers of women are in paid work, middle-class women are making some progress in the professions and, at the personal level, many women report enjoyment of the temporary respite from domestic isolation and drudgery which paid work can offer. However, the quantitative expansion of female employment gives little cause for celebration when we look at it in more detail.

Table 7 (p.97) lists the relative earnings of male and female manual and non-manual workers in 1983. It shows that, despite the equal pay legislation of 1975, women's average gross weekly earnings were only 65 per cent of men's. In 1979, the Low Pay Unit, operating on its definition of low pay being less than £1.50 per hour, found that 800,000 men and 2.5 million women were low-paid workers. P. Townsend's (*Poverty in the United Kingdom*,

1979) study of poverty in Britain found that women, and particularly single parents and elderly women, were predominant
among the poor. Illich (*Gender*, 1983) thinks that 'Pay is the one
measuring stick that counts', and he believes that the increasing
numbers of working women represents not a move towards
sexual egalitarianism, but rather little more than an increase in
exploitation.

Women's position in the occupational structure has not
changed very much either. It has three key characteristics. First,
much of women's work reflects their domestic role; the majority
of cleaners, cooks, clothes makers, infant teachers and nurses are
women. As has been argued already, domestic work has little
status, and paid work involving the same or similar tasks is
unlikely to have much more. Second, women predominate in
work roles which require deferential behaviour, such as waitres-
sing and shop work, which require the 'female' qualities of
politeness and responsiveness to the needs of others. Seeing
mainly women performing these roles does little to help revalua-
tion of those qualities or of the women themselves. Third, for
many women, paid work is another job added to their domestic
responsibilities; almost 60 per cent of married women are also in
paid employment. Any notion of these women competing fairly
and effectively with male workers is nonsensical unless their
husbands assume half the domestic responsibilities. These
women often seek undemanding and part-time work to ease this
double burden. Such work is rarely an avenue to promotion. We
will now look at this 'double shift' position.

The double shift and its effect on women's employment

Few women question their responsibility for home/child/
husband care, even when working full-time as well. Very few
men shoulder anything approaching half the work that keeps a
family functioning. A UNESCO study of daily time budgets
concluded:

> In no country do employed men spend more than half an hour
> in housework, and employed women less than an hour and
> half, even though women's working hours outside the home

are sometimes longer than men's.

E. Boulding in *Parity Begins at Home*, EOC/SSRC, 1981

Table 5 p.95 shows participation rates in a number of household activities by the husbands of working women in Sunderland.

The double shift has double consequences; not only can women not compete in the job market while they are performing two jobs, but also they may suffer discrimination from employers who are well aware that women have another full-time job to perform. They may therefore be less than willing to employ and promote women. Audrey Hunt (*Management Attitudes and Practices Towards Women at Work*, 1975) studied management attitudes toward women and described the family situation of those men who implemented personnel policy: Although 95 per cent were married, less than a third had wives in paid work and very few contributed to household management other than gardening, decorating or repairs. Hilary Land (*Parity Begins at Home*, 1981) notes that 'It would be surprising if their attitudes towards women combining paid employment with family responsibilities was not coloured in part by their own situation.' She also suggests that these men's attitudes would be unlikely to be sympathetic to any *man* who wished to adjust his working situation in order to share domestic responsibilities with his wife.

Such covert discrimination which may be practised by men who believe that married women make less than satisfactory workers, is described by Oonagh Hartnett as 'institutional sexism'. In Reading 8 (p.112) she reviews the research on these beliefs and is able to denounce them as 'myths'.

Some women workers' attempts to overcome the double-shift handicap may render them even more disadvantaged than other working women.

Britain's hidden army

This term has been coined to describe workers who perform paid work without entering the official labour force. This group, mainly women, are often housebound by their commitments to families where money is tight. Their solution is to work at home assembling small products such as Christmas crackers or transistor radios or sewing up clothes from pre-cut fabric. In 1979 the

Low Pay Unit included a questionnaire in its bi-monthly news-paper to these workers. The 49 women who replied were therefore a small sample and self-selected but the survey dis-closed that 30 per cent of the workers earned less than 20p an hour, 50 per cent less than 40p and 15 per earned £1.00 an hour or a little more. These wages had to cover the cost of heating and lighting the 'workplace' and the wear and tear that the work caused to the home. The benefits to employers from such workers include cheap labour, no overheads, no holiday or redundancy payments and exemption from National Insurance Contributions. There are estimated to be upwards of 150,000 such workers in the UK and the vast majority of them are women.

Approximately 43,000 more women work at home as child-minders. The Low Pay Unit's 1980 study of this group found the average earnings for a forty hour week to be £28.37 before deductions for the child's food and toys or wear and tear on the home. 85 per cent of these women offered their own childcare responsibilities as the reason they did this work but some also noted the service they rendered other women:

> I mind a child from a one-parent family and I think the social services should help in the financial field. I know they help in the way of benefits but if the parent earns more than the stated amount, the benefits are cut down, making life harder for the parent. My parent sometimes says she has no will to work because the harder she works the less she earns. And if she has no job neither do I.
>
> Childminder in *Berkshire Low Pay Unit pamphlet 17*,
> Angela Coulter, 1981

These women, then, are a particularly disadvantaged group of workers. The next section looks at women who find themselves out of the paid economy altogether.

Women and unemployment

Although women's jobs in the service sector offer then some measure of protection from the recession, there is evidence that unemployment is affecting women more than men. One reason is women's situation as part-time workers. Some 84 per cent of all part-time jobs are held by women and a common feature of collective redundancy agreements is that part-timers are the first to be laid off. The table below shows the relative male – female job losses in production and service industries and the percentages of part-time job losses.

Job losses by type of industry, 1981

	Men	*Women*	*Part-time Women*
Production industry	8.9%	12.7%	16.3%
Service industry	2.51%	2.48%	1.7%
	(July)	(July)	(March)

Source: Department of Employment Statistics, 1982

Once unemployed, women are less likely than men to receive state benefits. One reason for this is that married women have been allowed to pay half contributions to National Insurance, and their low pay encourages them to do this, but the reduced contribution renders them ineligible for benefit. In 1979 there were estimated to be 250,000 unregistered unemployed women. In 1981, a *New Statesman* article by Peter Kellner estimated that 'one million people, the great majority of them women', were not registered. Figure 5.1 shows the result of the General Household Survey on this issue.

It seems that newly unemployed women 'disappear' back into their housewife role. None of these figures include the large numbers of public employees, such as dinner ladies or cleaners in schools, who have had their working hours reduced by cuts in public spending. If these reduced hours amount to fewer than eight per week, the workers are then outside the scope of the Employment Protection Act.

The women who are most vulnerable to unemployment are those in part-time and/or routine, unskilled work which is most likely to be automated. The expanding areas of employment are the high-technology industries, which are still not attracting many women other than VDU operators or as operators of word processors. The implications for the education of women are enormous; unless schools and colleges make greater efforts to

Figure 5.1 Women and men not registered for unemployment benefit in the UK, 1974–80

The unemployed and the economically inactive but unregistered: males and married females

Year	Males		Married females	
	Percentage not registered	Base =100%	Percentage not registered	Base =100%
1974	15	281	77	99
1975	13	416	70	129
1976	10	533	63	168
1977	11	468	53	173
1978	11	451	56	171
1979	11	457	48	127
1980	11	623	43	182

Source: General Household Survey, 1980

encourage young women into science and technology, future prospects for women's employment look very depressing.

From this review of the situation of working women we turn to the various theoretical debates that attempt to explain their situation.

Ideology and social theory

We have noted elsewhere the tendency of social theorists to ignore women's unpaid work. The situation has been very similar regarding their paid work also, for industrial sociology and economics have paid scant attention to women employees until quite recently. However, a social change as great as the return of married women to paid employment in the last forty years could hardly go unnoticed. During the 1950s and 1960s, specialist studies of employed women began to appear, many of which were concerned to uncover the effect of women's paid work upon the family. A welter of media attention was given to the matter, there by reflecting and reinforcing the view that women's place was in the home and that working wives and mothers were in some way 'deviant'. In the same era there appeared many conflicting and contradictory studies which attempted to prove or disprove the hypothesis that the children of working mothers were 'deprived' (see also Readings 6 and 8 p.111 and 112). The inherent sexism of these approaches is best illustrated by considering how strange it would be to ask a *man* why he works! A sounder starting point might be to ask a woman not why she works but rather, 'why not?'.

The exclusion of women from paid work

Before industrialisation women played a full participatory role in economic life although Virginia Novarra (*Men's Work; Women's Work*, 1980) notes that women's work has always been in six spheres: childbearing, provision of food, provision of clothing, care of the sick, weak and elderly, responsibility for the nurture of children and cleaning. All but the first of these have at some time been part of the money economy. That is not to say that women have not always provided these services free for their families, but to emphasise the fact that until the eighteenth and nineteenth centuries, women played an active part in economic life. They did this through their participation in agriculture, textile work, and skilled trades. They did not have equality with men but, as Oakley explains:

> Women made good, if slightly cheaper sheep-shearers, hay-thatchers, harvesters, accountants and muck spreaders. Wives were not 'kept' but paid their own way by helping to support their families. Both husband and wife brought marketable skills and economic resources to their union.
>
> Ann Oakley, *Subject Women,* Martin Robertson, 1981

Industrialisation brought about the relocation of productive work. What once was produced in the home and community under the direction of senior males now was produced in factories, under the direction of capitalists. At first, the new mines, factories and mills offered paid work to women and children, although the workforce was often divided along sex lines, with women and children considered suitable only for

Fig. 5.2 Female labour and industrialisation

1 During the early industrial period, more workers equal-led more profit.

2 Women workers provided a cheap source of labour. Their 'nimble fingers' and 'ability to withstand boring, repetitive tasks' were seen as 'natural abilities', not skills to be financially rewarded.

3 Presumed dependence on a male justified paying women workers less.

4 A workforce divided on sex lines discouraged worker solidarity and depressed general wage levels. Braverman notes how labour is equalised and its power diminished by capital replacing old workers with young, skilled workers with unskilled and men with women.

certain types of activity. Figure 5.2 outlines the way this was advantageous to capital.

However, there was resistance from within and outside the workforce; social reformers expressed concern about appalling working conditions and speculated about their effect on women's reproductive functions, while male-dominated trade unions pressed for agreements which limited the use of female labour. (Reading 10, p.116, explains the exclusionary policies of some trade unions and Reading 11, p.117 shows female parti-cipation in unions today.) Meanwhile, the emerging and ex-panding professions were banning women from the practice of law, medicine and academic work, thereby denying paid work to middle-class women. Thus, women became marginalised in low-paid, unskilled trades, in casual labour and in governess and low-status teaching work, depending on their social class.

Hilary Land (in *The Woman Question*, 1982) notes that it was during the nineteenth century that the concept of the 'family wage' arose. This is a male wage which supports a whole family and supposedly justifies paying men more than women. Allied to this was the emergence of the decorative, idle wives of the newly rich, soon to become a desired, if not so easily attainable, ideal for the working and lower-middle classes.

Thus, there developed two distinct spheres of activity: the

public, waged work of the male and the private, unpaid domestic work of the female – supplemented where possible by low-status and often insecure employment. The primacy of women's domestic work prevented them from competing effectively in the labour market and the organisation and structure of industry made combination of the two roles almost impossible; the situation has changed relatively little since that time. Women were therefore in a very poor bargaining position and little union support prevented any improvement in their situation. Nevertheless, increasing numbers of married women have returned to work this century, particularly in the last forty years. The next section explains this development.

The return to paid employment

The process has been twofold. There have been structural changes which have 'pulled' women into the workforce, such as the boom in the service sector and the growth of the welfare state demanding women as typists, telephonists, nurses and so on, and 'push' factors, such as the fact that women now have longer periods of their life free from the demands of young children and

Fig. 5.3 The return to paid employment

1 Two world wars made it necessary to employ women to replace men away in the forces. Also the 'war economy' of the defence industries employed women.
2 Changes in industry, most notably the expansion of the service sector, led to the employment of women as telephonists, typists, clerks and so on.
3 Improved contraception released women from child-rearing for greater periods of their life.
4 The family wage has proved inadequate for many families' needs.
5 Increased expectations about material circumstances often necessitates a second wage.
6 Improved educational standards heighten women's aspirations; many women work because they want to.

that rising expectations of material comfort often necessitate a second wage. We should not forget either that nearly one million women are sole provider for their family or that Britain's supplementary benefit costs would triple if it were not for women's work supplementing the family wage. The issues are summarised in Figure 5.3 and in the documents section, Table 6 (p.96) shows the relative importance women workers give to the features that attract them to paid employment.

We now consider theories which attempt to explain women's position in the occupational hierarchy and their subsequent low pay and status.

The reserve pool of labour theory

This Marxist concept originally applied to the 'lumpen proletariat' who were on the fringes of industrialisation and who could be attracted into, and rejected from, the workforce as industries' needs changed. The term is now most often applied to women and immigrant workers. High levels of 'hiring and firing' are usually found in smaller companies with low unionisation rates. Such companies often employ large numbers of women. Because of their family commitments women are not geographically mobile and therefore their labour is still available when demand returns. Whilst out of work, women's dependence on men relieves the state of responsibility for them, and their own belief that paid work is 'secondary' plus their low levels of union activity offers little resistance to such practices.

However, as Irene Brueghel (in *The Woman Question*, 1982) points out, women's cheaper rates of pay should indicate *less* tendency to lay off and, she argues, the fact that women and men work in substantively different areas of employment means there is rarely a need to decide which sex to make redundant. She describes the theory as 'too simple'.

Perhaps the function of female labour is to depress general wage levels? We consider this issue in the next section.

Feminisation of labour theory

This theory rests upon the Marxist idea of capital accumulation.

As industrialisation progresses and competition increases, capital must find a way of lowering the *value* of labour power. One way of doing this is to 'de-skill' a job and offer it to women workers at a lower rate of pay. An example is clerical work, once an all male, middle-class occupation, now feminised through the introduction of typewriters, adding machines and, lately, word processors. But does feminisation of labour occur before or after de-skilling? Thompson notes:

> Women were responsible for pioneering computer programming. But once it gained in status, the work was redefined in creative terms and taken over by men. Only when such tasks later became subject to de-skilling were women allowed to enter the occupation they had created.
>
> Paul Thompson, *The Nature of Work,* Macmillan, 1983

Others suggest that cases of women taking over the de-skilled jobs of men are rare and that jobs are, rather, sex segregated at their inception:

> Occupations are formed at times when technical and social changes (such as new inventions or changes in the supply of labour) effect changes in the social division of labour. The restructuring of the production process, or parts of it, takes particular forms which are the result of conflicts and struggles. At the same time that particular sets of work tasks are (re)grouped into occupations and that these are (re)defined in terms of skill, wage rates etc., I suggest these occupations are assigned (explicitly or implicitly) to workers of one or other sex. Once an occupation has been 'sex-typed', normative and other forces operate which maintain segregation,
>
> Linda Murgatroyd, *Gender and Occupational Statification,*
> Lancaster Regional Group, 1982

The same author notes that during this century men have made greater inroads into female occupations than vice versa. Table 9, (p.99,) provides evidence of this.

Thompson (*The Nature of Work,* 1983) believes that Marxist economic theory explains 'little about the structures and processes – linked to the family and patriarchy – which determine the use of female labour', and he stresses the need for attention to be given to 'the relationships of patriarchy and capital'.

The relationships of patriarchy and capital

A generation of feminist scholars have been suggesting that 'the determinate social formation is patriarchy' (Anthias). Hartmann (in *The Unhappy Marriage of Marxism and Feminism,* 1981) suggests that through their control of women, men learned the methods of domination and hierarchical organisation and then applied these techniques to the capitalist mode of production. For now, let us consider the possibility that *both* structures – patriarchy and capitalism – benefit from women's subordinate role in paid work. Hartmann argues that patriarchy pre-dated capitalism, but was threatened by industrialisation which offered a free market for labour in which men and women came into direct competition for jobs. The response was to confine women to low-pay, low-status jobs which, in turn, increased their dependence on men. Figure 5.4 outlines the three-fold nature of the benefits to patriarchy and capitalism.

It must be said that the process by which women were relegated to their position in the world of work is still a matter of great debate. We will return to that debate in the final section of the last chapter. We now consider occupational stratification models and assess the degree to which they are a useful analytical tool for understanding the structure of female labour.

Occupational stratification by sex

There are two key points to remember about *where* we find most women workers: the first is that they are overwhelmingly concentrated in just three areas – clerical (filing clerks and secretaries), personal service (hairdressers, shop assistants) and professional and technical (nurses and teachers). Table 8 (p.98) shows the percentages of women workers in these and other jobs. Secondly, *within* these occupations women are mostly to be found at the lower levels of status and pay. Any erosion of sex-typing seems to have benefited males more than females, as shown in Table 9 (p.99). For example, whilst only 9 per cent of the total number of nurses are men, they comprise 33 per cent of senior nursing staff. The teaching profession is another example. Far more females than males qualify as teachers but men achieve the university and administrative posts. It has been suggested,

Fig. 5.4 Women's work – Benefits to patriarchy and capital

	Benefit to patriachy	*Benefit to capital*
1 Women provide cheap, expendable pool of labour.	Increases their dependence on men; increases male control.	Cheap labour when required.
2 Women perform unpaid domestic labour.	Benefits and assists male workers.	Capital bears only the cost of productive labour. Cost of reproductive labour borne by male's wage.
3 The 'privatised' nuclear family becomes the market place for the products of capitalism.	Ideology of domesticity increases dependence on men.	Women undertake low-paid insecure work to secure consumer durables. Working women stimulate capital in domestic appliance, fast food industries etc.

Source: Adapted from H. Hartmann in 'Capitalism, Patriarchy and Job Segregation by Sex', *Signs*, vol. 1, no. 3, 1976

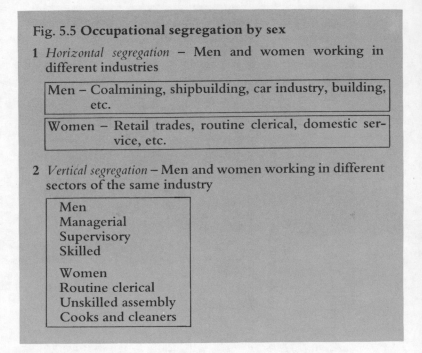

Fig. 5.5 Occupational segregation by sex

1 *Horizontal segregation* – Men and women working in different industries

> Men – Coalmining, shipbuilding, car industry, building, etc.

> Women – Retail trades, routine clerical, domestic service, etc.

2 *Vertical segregation* – Men and women working in different sectors of the same industry

> Men
> Managerial
> Supervisory
> Skilled
>
> Women
> Routine clerical
> Unskilled assembly
> Cooks and cleaners

therefore, that there are two types of occupational segregation by sex. Figure 5.5 shows this diagramatically.

Such a model goes some way to avoiding the mistaken assumption that men and women are in equal competition for jobs.

Let us now consider one theory which attempts to explain why women remain at the bottom of the structure. Human Capital Theory explains women's inferior position by their lower educational attainment and their interrupted careers. The former feature was discussed in Chapter 3. The effect of interruptions for childbearing can be seen in Figure 5.6, taken from a study of working–class women returning to work after their first and subsequent children.

It is clear that even within the working class considerable downward mobility occurs when women try to combine motherhood and work.

However convincing Human Capital Theory appears to be, it

Figure 5.6 Social class of women returning to work after childrearing

	First returners	Second or subsequent returners
Intermediate occupations	1.0	–
Skilled non-manual	20.2	8.5
Skilled manual	–	4.2
Semi-skilled manual	40.4	35.2
Unskilled manual	38.5	52.1
	100%	100%
	N=104	N=74

Source: Social Networks and Job Information: the situation of women who return to work, EOC and SSRC, 1981

does imply that women who acquire equivalent educational qualifications and who have no children enjoy equal occupational opportunity with men. Certainly, a minority of such women do achieve in the 'men's world' of, say, engineering or management, but that term in itself indicates the degree to which jobs are sex-typed before men and women compete for them. Indeed, it may be the sex of the occupant of a work role that determines its pay and status, rather than the intrinsic nature of the work itself. For these reasons, recent critiques of occupational stratification theory have questioned the validity of models which appear to be gender-free or neutral, for the sex of the worker has an important *determining* effect on a job's position in the occupational structure.

Occupational Stratification Theory makes a primary division of occupations into manual and non-manual. However, this poses a number of problems when women workers are also included. Firstly, even within the manual and non-manual categories, women are concentrated at the lower levels of each group. Secondly, there exists a considerable degree of overlap between male manual and non-manual workers in terms of pay, status and prestige. Thirdly, there are greater differences between the pay of men and women than there are between manual workers and non-manual workers (this is shown in Table 7 (p.97). Without consideration of these factors, present occupational stratification theory and theories such as the convergence thesis which attempts to explain point two (above), are less than valid unless they take male and female differentials into account.

Women and social mobility

Ignoring the unique features of women's position in paid work as well as ignoring their domestic work also makes assessment of women's social mobility extremely difficult. Most mobility studies have concentrated on men. For example, Halsey, Heath and Ridge explain women's absence from their influential study, *Origins and Destinations* (1980), by claiming that they did not include women because none of the previous studies had done so. This seems absurd, to say the least, but perhaps we should remember the problems which face the non-sexist researcher who tries to use existing models. In researching women's mobility, with whom do we compare women? Certainly not with her father if, as it seems, women are rarely in competition for the same jobs as men. With her mother? Definitely not if her mother was a housewife, for she will not appear in the model at all. No wonder women are omitted from large-scale mobility studies. Eichler (1980) believes that 'clearly we must start to reconceptualise our entire statification models'. That reconceptualisation and the reconstruction of work it will entail is a daunting task, for it will have to include sex as a variable of occupational segregation *and* include women's unpaid work. The implications for the re-analysis of both women's work *and* men's work are enormous. Perhaps a reader of this text will volunteer to make it their life's work?

This chapter closes by drawing together the various strands of the first section and assessing the potential for improving women's current position.

The future?

Virginia Novarra (*Men's Work; Women's Work*, 1980) lists the impediments to equal opportunities for women, and from these we may draw our own conclusions about possible policy changes. Firstly, she notes the lack of political will to effect change. An economy which benefits from women's unpaid domestic and low-paid labour is likely to be resistant to change. She suggests that it would involve 'programmes at least as large as those required to mobilise a workforce in times of war'. A second obstacle is the unwillingness of some men to relieve the situation at work and at home. Without a fairer division of domestic labour, equal opportunities programmes can benefit only a tiny minority of women. Thirdly, there is an inadequate theoretical and ideological base from which to begin any valid analysis of women's position in the occupational structure. Feminist academics have made some headway (see Chapter 7), but it is an enormous venture and some of the work still awaits academic respectability. The fourth impediment is the extreme polarisation of the sexes now. It is almost as if the gap has widened to a point where it is too wide to bridge, at least without substantial effort and will from social theorists, politicians and every member of the workforce. Finally, Novarra notes the global lack of expertise in the exercise of equal opportunities programmes. She suggests that an international effort is needed to exchange and share theory and practice.

I would like to make two points at the close of this chapter. The first is that this chapter has not discussed those ways in which women are handicapped before entry to paid labour; these are described in Chapter 3. Secondly, I fully acknowledge that I have not discussed the particular problems encountered by immigrant women. That would require another chapter, at least. For now, as a starting point, I simply offer the suggestion that immigrant women experience all the problems described here, and that these are further compounded by race.

6 A cross-cultural perspective

Women are 50 per cent of the world's population, put in two-thirds of the world's working hours, receive 10 per cent of the world's income and own less than 1 per cent of the world's property.

Oxfam Public Information Service, 1982

Examination of other cultures does indeed seem to reveal what Stanworth describes as 'the ubiquity of male domination'. Sex divisions exist in all societies but a universal form to female subordination is harder to find; there is no single way in which women are accorded second-class status and no constant pattern of behavioural expectation. Reading 6 (p.111), for example, shows that childrearing is not always considered the primary role of the natural mother. However, it does appear that most societies accord men more power to define their own and women's lives, and to control or limit women's experience as a means of sustaining that power. According to Weber, (*Economy and Society*, 1968), *power* means the ability to carry out one's will even when resisted by others, and in this respect there is substantial evidence to suggest that, in most cultures, women lack power. Later in this chapter we question the use of that term, and see how the perspective of the analyst, as well as the methodology of the researcher, ultimately affect the conclusions reached by social theorists. In other words, it is necessary also to look at *female power,* and ask whether a neuter use of the term power is valid for understanding the position of women. The first part of this chapter will accept a 'neuter' definition and attempt to describe and account for the universal existence of female subordination.

Degrees of female power

Leghorn and Parker (1981) have made a useful classification of societies by assessing the amount of control women have within them. Acknowledging that few societies fit neatly into any one category, they believe that three types of society exist. The first are *minimum power* societies where women have virtually no control over their own lives. The second are *token power* societies, where women are 'allowed' some freedoms, such as the theoretical and legal possibility of equality with men, but where such freedoms are ultimately dependent on a male dominated political and economic superstructure. The third type are *negotiating power* societies where women have influence and control which cannot be taken away by men. An example of each can be found in Reading 12 (p.118). Leghorn and Parker note, however:

> All three of these categories exist within a basic patriarchal context. Even in societies where women hold negotiating power and have (or have had) a higher status than in any other cultures we know of, men still subtly or overtly hold the greater prerogative in all areas and women still service men in the home free of charge.
>
> Leghorn and Parker, *Woman's Worth; sexual economics and the world of women,* Routledge and Kegan Paul, 1981

What then, is the basis of patriarchy? Where did men get their power? How is it sustained? We examine this next.

Power through violence

This argument rests on the assumption that men are 'naturally' stronger and more aggressive and that they use this physical superiority to ensure submission of the 'weaker' sex. Even in Western cultures which disapprove of the use of physical force in social life, 25 per cent of violent crime takes place within a heterosexual relationship, 40 per cent of women seeking divorce cite physical abuse as the grounds and Women's Aid Centres help more than 25,000 battered women each year and regularly appeal for more funds and centres. When it is remembered that these figures tell us nothing about women who remain quiet about a violent relationship, serious doubts are raised about the belief that violence toward women constitutes little more than isolated examples of individual pathology.

Silence also shrouds the incidence of female infanticide in

societies where a girl child will prove a financial burden and where her marriage will cost the family a dowry and undesirable division of land:

> In 1855, Commander Moore commenced his tour of 322 villages and was 'convinced of the prevalence of (female infanticide) in at least 308 of them.' In 62 of these villages there was not a single girl below the age of six.
>
> Lalita Panigrahi, *British Social Policy and Female Infanticide in India,* Munshiram Manharlal, 1972

Between the fourteenth and eighteenth centuries, some seven million European women were burned as witches; most were midwives and healers and therefore posed a threat to the male-dominated Catholic Church and the emerging medical profession.

It does seem, then, that women who threaten the interests of men can indeed be 'put down', sometimes permanently. This led Simone de Beauvoir (*The Second Sex,* 1949) to speculate 'For a man to feel in his fists his will to self-affirmation is enough to ensure him of his sovereignty.'

Another type of violence occurs with female collusion and usually involves some cultural definition of beauty. Thus, Victorian women strapped themselves into boned corsets which damaged their internal organs and Chinese girls had their feet tightly bound to prevent them growing more than a desirable three or four inches. These definitions of beauty all involve considerable restriction of movement; tight skirts and high-heeled shoes may perform the same function today.

In parts of Africa, Australia, South America and South East Asia women's sexual freedom is sometimes curtailed through the practice of infibulation which involves the almost total closure of a girl's sexual organs, or clitoridectomy which involves the removal of the clitoris.

We began this section by suggesting that power over women may be achieved by man's superior physical strength; violence against women can also be seen as the ultimate expression of women's subordination. Another means of expressing female subordination is found in practices which limit female's freedom of movement or speech. We will consider these next.

Power through segregation

The exclusion of women from public life is widespread enough to be seen as a major form of social control. Many societies define women as the property of their fathers and husbands and proscribe all activities outside that relationship. The most extreme example can be found in the Arab world, where some 200 million women live in purdah; wives and daughters are confined to the home and allowed outside only when heavily veiled. One Moroccan woman described it:

> The veil, so talked about by tourists seeking exotic excitement around the Mediterranean shores, is the symbol of our slavery. The veil means that the woman belongs to a man who possesses her body and worries about it being seen by others. To a veiled woman, seclusion is the only rational way of life. Her only reasons for being are to provide sex, children and good cooking.
>
> Fatima Mernissi, 'Veiled Sisters', *New World Outlook,*
> vol. 31, no. 8, 1971

Towards the end of this chapter we will consider another way of viewing 'the veil', which suggests that the seclusion it offers is a form of female power.

In Britain, the 1975 Sex Discrimination Act ended the formal exclusion of women from 'male' spheres, but laws do not change ideology; many women may still feel uncomfortable entering male territory, even that as innocent as the local pub.

Another form of segregation involves surrounding women's reproductive functions with myth and taboo. Some pre-developed societies banish their females to a menstrual hut during their periods; orthodox Jewish women are still required to observe niddah and withdraw from all contact with men during menstruation; British women can still be heard whispering furtively about 'that time of the month'. Similarly, in a country in which the *Sun* newspaper daily displays a semi-naked woman, it is still considered somewhat improper to breastfeed a baby in public!

Several theories suggest that men fear and envy women's power to create life and that their response is to diminish and control it. Regulation of women's freedoms and practices which place them in seclusion and isolation may act as deterrents to the collectivisation of women and their powers. The common occurence of customs and rituals which indicate this fear led anthropologist Ashley Montagu (*The Natural Superiority of Women*, 1968) to speculate that 'Man's drive to achievement can, at least in part be interpreted as an unconsciously motivated attempt to compensate for their lack of biological creativity.' Psychologist Karen Horney (*New Ways in Psychoanalysis*, 1939) described the same phenomena as 'womb envy'. Reading 13 (p.120) contains extracts from Sherry B. Ortner's paper, 'Is female to male as nature is to culture'. She proposes that woman's more conspicuous reproductive functions are seen by men as threatening their supremacy, particularly in man's drive to control natural forces; these functions must therefore be strictly controlled and so, by association, must women.

The explanations offered so far have, as their starting point, the different physiology of men and women. As such, they seem to offer little hope of change. The next section locates female subordination in cultural forces, particularly those which determine a society's economic system.

Power through economic necessity

Despite the lack of a universal form of male supremacy, all societies make some sex-based distinctions or role and behaviour. The French anthropologist Levi-Strauss (in *Man, Culture and Society*, 1960) claimed that these distinctions encouraged mutual dependence between the sexes and thus ensured heterosexuality and the survival of the species. Indeed, all societies impose some limits on sexual activity, and homosexuality is often perceived as a threat to social stability. Levi-Strauss also noted the almost universal taboo on incest, a taboo which necessitates the creation of sexual relationships, and thereby alliances, outside the kinship group. He believed that acts of exchange are fundamental to social life; we exchange words, stories, goods and, according to this theory, women. Females may be a unit of exchange between groups and the resultant benefits accrue to men. Arranged marriages involving a dowry provide illustration of this. Further, the children of these alliances promote inter-group harmony. Women, then, are a sort of 'social glue' which bonds groups and cultivates mutual interest. The main weakness of this account is that it fails to explain why it is women and not men who are exchanged and it does not adequately explain the inferior *status* of women.

Engels' theory goes some way to answering these questions by suggesting that the acquisition of private property brought about 'the world historic defeat of the female sex'. He believed that humans once lived in nomadic groups where sexual divisions existed but where there was not such a marked degree of sexual domination. As agricultural skills developed and permanent settlements were made, increasing productivity brought about a

Fig. 6.1 'The world historic defeat of women'
A new society appears . . . in which the family system is entirely dominated by the property system. . . the reckoning of descent through the female line and the right of inheritance through the mother were hereby overthrown and male lineage and right of inheritance from the father instituted . . . Such a form of the family shows the transition of the pairing family to monogamy. . . In order to guarantee the fidelity of the wife, that is the paternity of the children, the woman is placed in man's absolute power; if he kills her, he is but exercising his right. . .

The emancipation of women becomes possible only when women are enabled to take part in production on a large social scale, and when domestic duties require attention only to a minor degree. And this has become possible only as a result of modern large-scale industry, which not only permits the participation of women in production in large numbers, but actually calls for it and, moreover, strives to convert private domestic work also into a more public industry. . . full freedom in marriage can become generally operative only when the abolition of capitalist production, and of the property relations created by it, has removed all those secondary economic considerations which still exert so powerful an influence on the choice of partner.

Source: Friedrich Engels, *The Origin of the Family, Private Property and the State*, Moscow, Foreign Language Publishing House, 1969

surplus which facilitated the ownership of private property. In order to pass their property on, men needed to ensure the paternity of their children. This required considerable restriction of women's freedom. Domestic work became domestic confinement and men's more public activity was accorded higher status (see Figure 6.1).

Engels and Marx believed that increased participation in wage labour and the socialisation of domestic labour are prerequisites to female emancipation. However, patriarchy continues to flourish in societies where women participate in paid labour and in communist countries which profess to have abolished private property. However, these accounts do locate female subordination in material rather than biological forces and have allowed the development of further analysis, particularly by Marxist feminists.

We now look at the position of women in societies undergoing rapid social and economic transformation and assess the impact of these changes on women's lives.

Women in developing countries

Once colonised by the rich countries of the West, many third world nations are now independent and attempting to industrialise. Apart from their industrial development these countries often model their political and bureaucratic structures on Western models, and frequently maintain close links with the previous coloniser. (There are notable exceptions to this such as Tanzania and Cuba, but space will not allow detailed discussion of these differences here.)

Development brings changes similar to those which accompanied our own industrial revolution including the emergence of class stratification and a population shift from rural to urban areas. Leghorn and Parker outline how these changes affect women and suggest that the existence of patriarchy before industrialisation 'made it possible for Western based forms of sexual oppression to be superimposed' (see Figure 6.2).

Large multi-national companies enjoy the benefits of cheap female labour to be found in third world countries. Whereas the post-Second World War economic boom stimulated the employment of Commonwealth labour in Britain, recession and

Fig. 6.2 **How development affects women**

1 Women are left to cope alone with subsistence farming when men move into industry and the production of cash crops.

2 Urbanisation means that women lose their traditional forms of shared child-care and female support systems.

3 Increasing governmental control and centralisation forces women from some of their traditional trading work. For example, women fish traders in Ga, West Africa were unable to compete when the government moved the harbour and introduced refrigeration.

4 Early development offers women paid work but further technological changes frequently result in high female unemployment. At the turn of the century 45 per cent of Brazil's workforce was female; now it is 21 per cent.

Source: adapted from Leghorn and Parker, *Women's Worth*, Routledge and Kegan Paul, 1981

'high' wages now make it economically expedient to manufacture goods in the third world.

Although some women may benefit from access to paid work and from improved healthcare, contraception and abortion facilities, the majority of women in third world countries have neither the educational preparation nor the geographical mobility required to benefit from modernisation. For example, in Nigeria illiteracy among women is twice as high as it is among men. Fertility control is perhaps the key towards emancipation for third world women but this often presents woman with a personal and moral dilemma in countries where the Catholic Church opposes state population policies.

Competition or complementation?

Illich (1983) believes that both sexes suffer from 'sexist exploitation characteristic of industrial societies'. He describes how development prompts the polarisation of sex roles when men and women compete for the (supposedly) scarce resources of industrial society.

He compares this with pre-developed societies where sexual divisions of labour exist but where the different needs of men and women are accounted for and where male and female roles are of a dual, complementary nature. He describes this as 'the reign of gender'. Industrialisation ignores different gender needs, and women inevitably lose:

> While under any reign of gender women might be subordinate, under *any* economic regime they are *only* second sex. . . both genders are stripped and, neutered, the man ends up on top. . . Economic discrimination against women cannot exist without the abolition of gender and the social construction of sex. . . The barriers that keep women from privileged wage labour and the traps that lock them in the kitchen are explained in different ways in Japan and the USSR, but everywhere they are comparable in height and depth. . . Economic discrimination against women appears when development sets in.
>
> Ivan Illich, *Gender,* Marion Boyars, 1983

Illich also suggests that when Western anthropologists study pre-developed societies they observe gender-based divisions of labour, fail to note the complementary nature of such divisions and describe them as yet another instance of sexual oppression. Their reports therefore, are distorted by having Western male value-systems imposed upon them. 'Soon the work of several generations of anthropologists provided abundant evidence of an almost grotesque inability even to suspect what women do', claims Illich.

The problem of data collection and interpretation has important implications for the study of gender differences. We will look at these problems next.

Male bias in the social sciences?

In recent years feminist academics have analysed how social science has systematically ignored and distorted women's experience. This has been discussed in Chapters 3 and 4; this claim may now be studied with respect to anthropological work.

'Bringing women back in' is difficult without a theoretical framework, as Oakley points out:

> To make visible the invisible is *not a simple additive formula:* traditional history/sociology/economics/psychology/philosophy/anthropology/literature + women's studies = the whole story.

Ann Oakley, *Subject Women,* 1981

It is necessary to understand some of the methodological, theoretical and practical constraints which have hindered the development of a non-sexist social analysis and which must be overcome if we are to develop a paradigm which does more than just 'tag women on'.

Any observation of social life is affected by the observer's inability to suspend completely all previous experience and belief. As humans observing other humans our judgement is coloured by our own social and cultural experiences and these will affect the meanings we impute to any social phenomena we observe. Further, the experience of observation changes us and those whom we study; no human being can be a mere catalyst for value-free information and we must take this into account in the final analysis. The participant observer sees through culture-loaded vision and so do those who are being observed, for they too will impute motives and beliefs onto the researcher. In the same way that knowledge in schools is subject to a selection procedure, the parameters of 'worthwhile' study in the social sciences are set by certain influential individuals. The world-view of those individuals can have far reaching implications not only for what is considered a worthwhile subject for study but also for the way in which interpretations are offered.

Recent critiques have questioned the assumption that all women's work is of secondary importance or that their behaviour displays deference to men. To take a concrete example of this we might consider whether the veil of Arab women – described earlier in this chapter as a form of female exclusion – might not also be seen as a way in which *women* exclude *men*? It may afford women considerable privacy; no men are permitted to enter when a group of veiled women meet. However, veiled women are frequently present at male gatherings, albeit in the role of food-servers and so on.

Men dominate the social sciences, particularly in the spheres of theory and research; women in the profession have often had to concur with these men if they were to succeed. The situation is changing, as June Nash (in *Sex and Class in Latin America*, 1980) explains, 'The values on which our selective criteria are premised are being questioned by people who were never before a significant enough part of the profession to challenge them.'

When sociologists speak of power and of politics there is usually an unquestioning acceptance of the Aristotelian definition which links power and politics to public activity. If this definition is used then men do have more power than women. However, it is possible that tacit acceptance of *public power* as the yardstick with which to measure the relative position of women and men, makes analysis more a product of selective perception than the social reality it tries to describe. This is the theme of Ernestine Friedl's work, *The position of women: appearance and reality*, 1967. She argues that if, as it seems, sociologists regard the family as the most significant social unit (see Chapter 3), then the private, home-based power of women has more social importance than the public power of men. She described life in a Greek village and agrees that observed custom and practice can be interpreted as according men most power and privilege. In public places such as the village square and the church, women's behaviour is limited and segregated. There exists also a clear division of labour in the home but she notes that here neither male nor female activity is accorded higher status. From this point her account offers an alternative view to that which might be expected, for she pays particular attention to the power women wield by virtue of the land they bring as a marriage dowry, their continuing power over the distribution and use of that land and their power to organise the lives and activities of family members. Friedl also notices how women are capable of bringing dishonour on their menfolk by infringing the rules which circumscribe their public behaviour. All these factors, together with women's ability to control men through their complaints and reminders create a strong sense of obligation in the men of the village. Her interpretation then, challenges studies which are preoccupied with men's work, men's power and men's values:

> For the weaker partner in a social structure the ability to create and maintain a sense of obligation in the stronger is a real

exercise of power, and one in which Greek women are past masters (sic).

Ernestine Friedl in *The Woman Question,*
Mary Evans (ed.), Fontana, 1982

This work looked closely at women's lives, asked certain rather unusual questions and came up with a rather unusual analysis. Men might be more likely to ask other questions. Illich (1983) reminds us that men are also more likely to have the skills and expertise to undertake research work and, when 'in the field', might enjoy increased access to and rapport with the male members of the group being studied.

Joyce Pettigrew recalls a similar phenomenon in 'Reminiscences of fieldwork among the sikhs' (in *Doing Feminist Research,* 1981). As an anthropologist married to a Sikh man, her research into landowning Sikhs in the Punjab was handicapped by her inability to go out alone or address men without bringing disrespect upon herself or her husband's family. As a woman, certain information would have been withheld from her and she was forced to rely on the men in her family to act as intermediaries for her. She also claims that the focus of her research was determined by its academic acceptability. To have investigated the lives and work of women in her husband's family would, at the time, have been considered unsuitable material. It would have been seen as allowing feeling and personal experience to have interfered with the supposed value-free objectivity demanded of her. Her work, then, involved the adoption of what Oakley described as 'pseudo-masculinity'. Hochschild's comment that 'cognitive, intellectual or rational dimensions of experience (are defined as being) superior to being emotional or sentimental', may help us to understand the claim that the focus and methodology of the social sciences are defined in terms of a male-oriented value system. That is, public areas of social life are not only controlled by men but also studied (mainly) by men and defined by them as superior to domains where women have most influence and power. Throughout this text we have raised the issue of perspective and discussed whether sociological theory and method is confounded, even distorted, by whether we are males observing males, males observing females, females observing males or females observing females! This is certainly an important area of debate but within it there is also the implied critique that any sociological work that does not acknowledge and incorporate the lives of women *as experienced by women* is, by that omission, invalid. This is certainly a debate that is likely to continue for some time. David Morgan reviewed his own work in the light of such charges and also examined the implications of such claims for male researchers and for men in sociology:

> It is worth stressing. . . that this concern about sexism in sociological enquiry is a concern about scholarship. . . this is not just a matter of concern for those who happen to be interested in feminism or 'women's studies' but something that affects everyone engaged in sociological work. Sexist domain assumptions, in whatever specialised field of enquiry, do have consequences for the outcome of investigations and in many cases the final outcome would have been very different had the investigator taken account of questions of gender.
>
> David Morgan, 'Men, masculinity and sociological enquiry' in *Doing Feminist Research*, Helen Roberts (ed.), Routledge and Kegan Paul, 1981

Such issues reflect current sociology and feminist sociologies in that there is no clear overall paradigm, and this is likely to be so for some time to come. However, awareness of the inherent difficulties does encourage rigorous scrutiny of all sociological theory and method. We will continue this line of enquiry in the next chapter, where we consider the social climate in which contemporary feminism arose and introduce the reader to some of the diversity of feminist debate.

7 The women's movement and feminism

The women's movement in context: the personal is the political

Although there is space here to discuss only the contemporary movement it would be historically incorrect and morally unjustifiable not to acknowledge the work of other generations of women who have worked for women's freedoms. As has been noted, women's history has been very inaccessible until recently, but elsewhere in this text we acknowledge the work of Mary Astell and Mary Wollstonecraft in the seventeenth and eighteenth centuries respectively. Most readers will be aware of the work of the women's suffrage movement and the suffragettes at the turn of the century; fewer might be aware of the ways in which working-class women organised against their working conditions in the last century. Few history books explain how two of the major revolutions in history – the American War for Independence and the French Revolution – left women with considerably fewer legal freedoms than they had before. (Interested readers will enjoy Dale Spender's *Feminist Theorists* which traces feminist thought from 1640 to the present day.) Our focus here must be the economic, cultural and political climate in which the contemporary movement emerged.

Two of the greatest periods of social unrest this century have witnessed an accompanying re-definition of femininity. In the 1920s women dressed and behaved in ways which outraged their parents, and the 1960s produced a similar phenomenon. At this time women found some measure of sexual freedom in a moral climate which questioned whether marriage was the only place for sexual activity and when cheap, reliable contraception became readily available.

We might speculate whether this 'sexual revolution' represented just another form of oppression for women; it was not much of a freedom to hobble around in high-heeled boots and mini-skirts or to live in a liberal atmosphere which offered men more sex with less responsibility. However, the beginnings of the present movement can be traced to this time, for both working-class and middle-class women.

Young, radical women working for black civil rights campaigns in America were forced to examine their own subjugation when one of the campaign's leaders, Stokely Carmichael, stated that within civil rights campaigns a woman's place was 'prone'. Some women recall making tea and sealing envelopes while men took the glory on the platforms and leading the marches. Within the revolutionary and left-wing movements, women's subordination was being ignored:

> This contradiction was powerful enough to bring women like me in the revolutionary movement to a recognition of ourselves as women. . . we supported many of the feelings of '68. . . [but] I found myself in conflict in an increasing number of particular incidents, sexual banter, the whistling when women spoke, the way men divided us into two, either as comrades or as women they fucked. Once a man told me to stop being so 'effeminate'.
>
> Sheila Rowbotham, *Woman's Consciousness, Man's World,*
> Pelican, 1973

But it was not only young, middle-class women who felt the sharp edge of contradiction. The nuclear family placed home-based women in isolation, cut off from kinship support networks (see also Friedan (1963), Chapter 4). Women entering paid work found themselves, often for the first time, in the competitive, hierarchically-ordered workplace so much at variance with their experiences as wives and mothers. Employment did not alter their marital relationship; they were still expected to be responsible for domestic work and childcare and prevailing notions of femininity did not change. These women faced the reconciliation of two, quite conflicting, spheres of activity. As the divorce rate rose in the 1970s increasing numbers of women faced the awesome responsibility of trying to be mother, father and breadwinner whilst the mass-media encouraged them to look beautiful and keep their homes immaculate at the same time. These changes and contradictions raised questions about the role of women and the female stereotype.

The late 1960s witnessed a new mood of militancy among the

Labour movement and whilst women workers were generally not as active as their male colleagues, many women joined campaigns for better pay and conditions. Then, in 1968, women sewing machinists at Ford's went on strike demanding regrading of their work; they were paid at unskilled rates whilst their male colleagues received skilled rates of pay. The women did not get regraded but did achieve a new rate at 95 per cent of the men's.

Structural changes had thrown women's position into relief; the forces of capitalism which some two hundred years previously, had contributed to their relegation to unpaid or low-paid work, now acted as agents of change in their lives. Apart from joining the paid work force, women now had some measure of control over their fertility and domestic technology offered them some relief from household drudgery. General levels of education were higher too and women began asking some very searching questions about their roles and status. The Women's Movement, with its support groups, campaigns and emerging theories began addressing these questions.

Some of the changes demanded by feminists have far-reaching implications for family life; a major difference between today's movement and earlier feminism is that the former is highly critical of existing family structures and ideologies of sex role. Jean Gardiner notes that 'domestic labour did not even exist as a theoretical category before the current feminist movement made it into an area of theoretical and political debate' (*New Left Review* no. 89, 1975).

Perhaps it is only in the late twentieth century, when biological reproduction can be controlled and when the socialisation of housework and childcare is a theoretical possibility, that such challenges to existing structures and ideologies can be offered. Before reviewing some of the current issues of debate we will consider some of the issues which feminists see as contributing to women's oppression, and look at the specific action being taken against them.

Issues identified and action taken

In order to understand the campaign groups which have emerged it is necessary to clarify what are seen to be the main barriers to female liberation. Today's movement identifies 'the

Fig. 7.1 Issues identified and action taken

Women are:	*Women organise:*
unpaid or underpaid for their work	Rights for Women unit of NCCL Equal Pay and Opportunity Campaign Working Women's Charter Groups Women's Advisory Committee
discriminated against for their reproductive functions and lacking adequate control over those functions	Mothers in Action Group Women's Health Collectives National Abortion Campaign Campaign against VAT on sanitary protection Association of Radical Midwives Maternal Defence Fund
ideologically represented as inferior	Women's Media Action Group Women's Broadcasting and Film Lobby Pornography is Violence Against Woman Campaign
vulnerable to and inadequately protected from attack by men	Rape in Marriage Campaign Women Against Violence Against Women Reclaim the Night Campaign Women's Aid Federation Rape Crisis Centres
excluded from valued activities	Women's Campaign for Jobs Girls into Science and Technology Girls and Mathematics Project Women in Publishing

Source: adapted from Penelope Brown, 'Universals and particulars' in *Women in Society*, Virago, 1981

family household system' and an ideology which devalues
women and endorses their role as unpaid domestic workers as
the two key contributors to female subordination. In Figure 7.1
are listed more specific issues and the campaigns which have
formed in response. It is by no means an exhaustive list, merely
an indication of the range of action taken over the last twenty
years. It is an ethnocentric account for it fails to include
campaigns on issues confronting women in other cultures. We
should also remember that some campaigns are contentious; for
example 'Wages for Housework' could serve to reinforce the
belief that women should be responsible for housework and
childcare.

We turn next to the two main strands of feminist theory. They
are by no means as mutually exclusive as they at first appear and
this account cannot do justice to the wide diversity of opinion
within each perspective.

Feminism: theory, policy and politics

Radical feminism

Radical feminism developed in response to the lack of theoretical tools with which to analyse women's oppression. Radical
feminists find Marxist theory intellectually disappointing for it
offers little explanation of patriarchy. From disillusion with
economic class analysis came the proposition that women con-
stitute a separate class by nature of their subordination to men.
This may be compounded by economic class but attempts to
assess the position of women through conventional stratification
theory is seen to be an essentially androcentric enterprise. In
1969, the Redstockings of New York included the following in
their manifesto:

> We cannot rely on existing ideologies as they are all products
> of a male supremacist culture. We question every generalisa-
> tion and accept none that is not confirmed by our own
> experience. We identify with all women.

Quoted in Coote and Campbell, *Sweet Freedom*, Picador, 1982

Such subjectivity raises questions about all methodologies and
theories but does enable us to 'bring women back in' and

encourages very close scrutiny of all social theory for sexist assumptions.

Radical feminism argues that patriarchy underpins every social relationship. S. Firestone (*The Dialectic of Sex*, 1972) posited a theory of how this might have come about: women's reproductive functions have made them dependent on men for much of human history. As women learned to control their fertility and to find alternative forms of support, men learned the techniques to ensure their domination. These were the creation of an ideology which stresses conformity to sharply divided gender roles and an economic system which perpetuates women's financial dependence on men. She believed that liberation would be attained only when reproduction is achieved artificially and when machines replace human labour, freeing men, women and children to live as equal social beings.

For radical feminists the revolution is now; theory and practice are inseparable. In Reading 14 (p.121) Gail Chester outlines some of what this means to her. Men are seen as the oppressors who will not easily relinquish their power over women. Sheila Rowbotham, a socialist feminist, described how even men who support other campaigns for liberty and equality 'are like creatures who have just crawled out of their shells after millennia of protection'. It is not easy for men who see themselves as champions of the oppressed to re-view themselves as the oppressor! Although Rowbotham disagrees with separatism, she acknowledges the difficulty of overcoming internalisations of sex domination:

> When a man curls his lip, when he uses riducule, when he grows angry, you have touched a raw nerve in domination. Men will often admit other women are oppressed but not you. . . They will say you criticise the behaviour of men in a personal rather than a political way. If you are working class they'll humiliate you with your sex and class ignorances, if you are middle class they'll call you a petty bourgeois deviationist.
>
> Sheila Rowbotham, *Women's Consciousness, Man's World*,
> Pelican, 1973

Some radical feminist women find such struggles intolerable and they choose to exclude men as much as possible from their lives. Heterosexual relationships, romantic love and the idealisation of family life may be seen as ways of ensuring male control of women, and women who believe this may choose 'political' lesbian relationships instead; relationships with men being regarded as fraternisation with 'the enemy'. They also suggest that exclusive man–woman relationships divide women by petty jealousy and competition for males, thereby precluding female solidarity and collective action.

Socialist feminism

Before we review the socialist feminist debate we will assess their critique of radical feminism. Most of these criticisms are concerned with the biological determinism implicit when some radical feminists link women's subordination to their reproductive functions or when they suggest that male and female psychology is sufficiently different to allow the development of a 'power psychology' in the male. Such an emphasis might lean towards a fatalistic acceptance that relations between the sexes are incapable of change and fail to concentrate on why the characteristics of one sex are accorded higher value. It prompts research which ignores class and race as variables of female subordination and denies the often genuine love and cooperation that can exist between men and women.

British feminism has always been more socialist than its American counterpart because Britain has a long established tradition of left-wing activity in the Labour Party and trade unions; it was through such organisations that many British women came to feminism. Whilst there exists a danger that the understanding of women's oppression becomes lost in the struggle for class analysis, many socialist feminist theories have described female subordination within capitalism and have refined Marxist categories in the process. In particular, the role of ideology has been examined and it is on this area of interest that radical and socialist feminism finds a broad measure of agreement. To understand this we need to appreciate some later developments of Marxist theory, particularly those which describe how conflicts or contradictions which threaten the stability of capitalism may be 'managed' by promoting the values of the bourgeoisie until they become embedded in the very consciousness of *all* individuals.

Althusser asserts that ideology 'represents in its necessarily imaginary distortions not the existing relations of production (and the other relations that derive from them) but above all the (imaginary) relationship of individuals to the relations of production and the relations that derive from them'. (L. Althusser, 'Ideology and Ideological State Apparatuses in Cosin (ed.), *Education, Structure and Society*, Penguin, 1972). These imaginary distortions are disseminated via the 'Ideological State Apparatus' of the mass-media, religion, law and education. Although Althusser did not discuss ideological representations of women it is easy to use these concepts to show how ideology supports and reinforces women's subordination. Through the Ideological State Apparatus gender divisions come to be regarded as 'natural' or 'inevitable'; they become part of self identity and therefore highly resistant to change.

The politics of socialist feminism demands no withdrawal from 'male spheres', indeed, it is considered that it is from and within these arenas that female oppression must be fought. Nevertheless, the problem of how to incorporate feminist theory into the 'sex-blind' categories of Marxism remains. Michele Barratt acknowledges these difficulties in her work *Women's Oppression Today*. (See Table 11, p.103 for an overview). She is convinced that the development of capitalism did not need a particular form of family household system but that family

Figure 7.2 The family household system

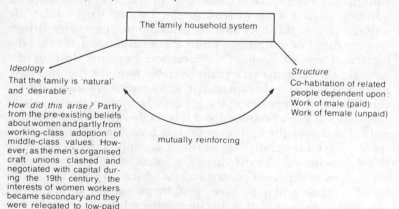

The family household system

Ideology
That the family is 'natural' and 'desirable'.

How did this arise? Partly from the pre-existing beliefs about women and partly from working-class adoption of middle-class values. However, as the men's organised craft unions clashed and negotiated with capital during the 19th century, the interests of women workers became secondary and they were relegated to low-paid or unpaid work.

mutually reinforcing

Structure
Co-habitation of related people dependent upon:
Work of male (paid)
Work of female (unpaid)

Source: adapted from Michele Barrett, *Women's Oppression Today*, Verso Edns, 1980

relationships which existed prior to the Industrial Revolution have been moulded to suit a capitalist economy and are now an integral part of it. There now exists, she believes, 'a fundamental relationship between the wage labour system and the organisation of domestic life'. Figure 7.2 shows how this system endures by its structure and the ideology which surrounds it.

The results, says Barratt, are as follows:

1 Women's poor bargaining position in paid work and their unpaid role as domestic workers consolidate their inferior position in both spheres.
2 The working-class is divided on sex lines. Although working-class men made some short-term gain from the marginalisation of female labour, it was capital which made most gain. They may have lost some economic gain from not having women in waged production but they increased political power from the sex division. This power was consolidated by legislation which purported to protect women but which in fact increased their dependence on men.
3 The system that emerged restricted male workers also by 'trapping' them in wage labour for their families, precluded close contact with their children and imposed rigid definitions of masculinity on them.

Barrett believes that organised labour has not opposed this situation because of sex-role ideology. As we described earlier, Barrett believes that gender ideology becomes part of our sense of self: 'Gender identity and the ideology of the family are embedded in our very subjectivity.' If this is so, proposals for change which threaten beliefs about the family will also threaten sexual identity and be rejected. Nevertheless, she believes that female liberation is possible within capitalism by:

1 A redivision of childcare and domestic responsibility.
2 An end to the assumption that women are dependent upon men.
3 A transformation of the ideology of gender.

In their critique of Barrett's work, Johanna Brenner and Maria Ramas claim that she failed to address the question of why the drive to capital accumulation (the tendency for capital to appropriate all forms of work, including women's domestic work) coupled with the realities of male oppression, have not threatened 'the family household system'. They claim that her recourse to 'the ideology of gender' invests it with an autonomy that is far from proven. They challenge the historical accuracy of her account of the trade unions' exclusionary policies in the nineteenth century, and believe that women's biological functions cannot be ignored in the analysis, although they accept that this can be a 'heretical' stance for socialist feminists. They suggest that women's reproductive functions played a critical role in their subordination; women's productive work before industrialisation had been tailored to accommodate their domestic responsibilities but the factory system put the two spheres of work in conflict. Employers were unwilling to make allowances for women's family responsibilities, and the low wages of workers made alternative forms of domestic help and childcare impossible. Women's 'domestication' and their marginal role in paid work was, therefore, 'inevitable'. The material forces of production are 'an inescapable social reality'; the day-to-day experiences and demands of working-class life are as much a shaping feature of ideology as any bourgeois construction of reality, they claim:

> Because the family household system imposed itself on individuals with unrelenting logic, women and men had to take these social relationships into account when forming their ideas about themselves and their world. That was true not only for the bourgeoisie but also for the working class. . . Far more than equal pay would have been necessary in order to construct a non-patriarchal form of reproducing the working class.
>
> Johanna Brenner and Maria Ramas,
> 'Rethinking women's oppression', *New Left Review*, 144,
> March/April 1984

These are demanding arguments and the point of presenting them here is not to confuse the student; it is, rather, to introduce some of the complexities of feminist analysis in the last twenty years. The theoretical dilemmas faced by feminist academics are described in Reading 15 (p.123). Such work cannot help but contribute to a reworking of all sociological theory and method.

In his discussion of the 'fragmentory' effect of the perspectives approach to advanced level sociology, O'Donnell (*A New Introduction to Sociology*, 1981) raises the issue of a more unified paradigm. He did not argue for the inclusion of feminist perspectives in his argument, but I suggest that such an inclusion would have very much the same effect: 'a collective enterprise. . . would be painful and would involve laying to rest numerous sociological fables and exorcising not a few sociological ghosts.' I would like to suggest that a sociology without its patriarchal ghosts and its fables about women would be a far sounder sociology.

What is feminism? The implications for sociology

> Ultimately any feminism is about putting women first; it is about judging women's interests (however defined) to be important and to be insufficiently represented and accommodated within mainstream politics/academia.
>
> Ann Oakley, *Subject Women,* 1981

I offer that definition fully aware that it is open to the charge of sexism for it implies putting men second. However, the volume of work that has come from female academics in the movement should help convince young social scientists that sociology, like the world it describes and explains, has been, from the founding fathers (sic) onwards, largely the work of men who have offered interpretations from their perspectives as men. Sociologists, no less than the groups they study, are likely to use what Schutz described as 'cook book knowledge'. That is, we all use tried and tested recipes to explain the world to ourselves and others. The social world attaches great importance to male principles and that is how explanations of it emerge. Where sociology has not ignored women it has examined them as a separate category which deviates from the male 'norm'. Why else would there be a need for a text like this, if women were not treated as a separate 'category' in the syllabus?

Only by 'putting women first' may we redress that imbalance and correct a structural flaw in our discipline. It was the feminist academics who noticed the flaw when they searched for explanations of the 'contradictions' in women's lives. They now find themselves with the daunting task of forging new theories. The problems involved are outlined in Reading 15 (p.123). Meanwhile, Delamont has described how we must begin:

> More women should engage in research and teaching. . .

research should be conducted into all aspects of women's lives. . . all social science theory and research should be rigorously scrutinised for implicit and explicit assumptions about women.

Sara Delamont, *The Sociology of Women*,
Allen and Unwin, 1980

PART 3

Statistical data and documentary readings

---

8 Statistical data

Table 1 Sex role ideology in children's reading schemes

The table on page 88 shows stereotypical sex-role behaviour attributed to characters in six popular British reading schemes. The author believes 'The schemes. . . concentrate on the exploits of males. . . and the stories in the schemes cannot but reinforce the damage that our society does to girls' self-esteem'.

Tables 2 a,b,c Statistical data on achievement and destinations of male and female students

Tables 2a–2c (pp.89–90) show pass rates in the major subjects in years 1970–1979. Decreased participation of girls in full-time education can be clearly seen at post-sixteen and again at post-eighteen. In 1979 girls received 50.8 per cent of all GCE passes at O-level and 43.8 per cent at A-level which reflects a certain measure of progress over the last decade. However, there is still a clear pattern of girls qualifying in predominantly arts and social science subjects as opposed to physical sciences, mathematics and technical subjects. Although girls have been increasing their representation in chemistry, physics and mathematics, they appear to be making relatively little headway in computer science.

Table 1 The sex-roles that occurred in three or more of the six schemes coded

The sex for which the role was prescribed	The content of the children's roles				The adult roles presented
	Toys and pets	Activities	Taking the lead in both sex activities	Learning a new skill	
Girls only	1 Doll 2 Skipping rope 3 Doll's pram	1 Preparing the tea 2 Playing with dolls 3 Taking care of younger siblings	1 Hopping 2 Shopping with parents 3 Skipping	1 Taking care of younger siblings	1 Mother 2 Aunt 3 Grandmother
Boys only	1 Car 2 Train 3 Aeroplane 4 Boat 5 Football	1 Playing with cars 2 Playing with trains 3 Playing football 4 Lifting or pulling heavy objects 5 Playing cricket 6 Watching adult males in occupa-tional roles 7 Heavy gardening	1 Going exploring alone 2 Climbing trees 3 Building things 4 Taking care of pets 5 Sailing boats 6 Flying kites 7 Washing and polishing Dad's car	1 Taking care of pets 2 Making/Building 3 Saving/Rescuing people or pets 4 Playing sports	1 Father 2 Uncle 3 Grandfather 4 Postman 5 Farmer 6 Fisherman 7 Shop or business owner 8 Policeman 9 Builder 10 Bus driver 11 Bus conductor 12 Train driver 13 Railway porter
Both sexes	1 Book 2 Ball 3 Paints 4 Bucket and spade 5 Dog 6 Cat 7 Shop	1 Playing with pets 2 Writing 3 Reading 4 Going to the seaside 5 Going on a family outing	—	—	1 Teacher 2 Shop assistant

Source: Glenys Lobban, 'Sex Roles in Reading Schemes' in *Sexism in Children's Books*, Writers and Readers Publishing Cooperative, 1976

Table 2a Females as a percentage of GCE O-level passes (A-C grades only),
selected subjects (summer examinations). England and Wales, 1970-79

Subject	1970	1975	1979
Technical drawing	0.4	1.5	2.7
Physics	20.9	21.8	25.0
Computer studies	—	—	27.4
Chemistry	28.9	31.9	35.9
Economics	34.4	36.6	37.8
Mathematics	37.5	38.7	41.0
Geography	44.4	43.7	42.9
History	52.9	49.5	50.9
English language	56.6	56.8	57.6
Biology	64.5	59.8	59.5
French	56.7	58.6	60.0
German	58.2	59.3	60.7
English literature	61.4	60.9	61.9
Sociology	—	71.8	75.4
Cookery	99.3	98.8	98.2
All subjects	49.5	50.1	50.8

Table 2b Females as a percentage of GCE A-level passes in selected subjects
(summer examinations). England and Wales, 1970-79

Subject	1970	1975	1979
Technical drawing	0.5	0.8	1.8
Physics	16.7	18.2	18.9
Computer studies	—	—	19.3
Mathematics (pure and applied)	17.6	22.4	24.6
Chemistry	24.7	29.1	30.6
Economics	18.6	24.0	31.1
Geography	41.4	40.7	41.2
History	49.6	49.4	50.4
Biology	48.8	49.4	53.0
French	64.4	67.9	65.5
German	60.5	66.4	62.9
English literature	63.6	66.8	69.7
Sociology	—	69.7	73.7
Domestic subjects	99.8	99.3	99.5
All subjects	40.4	43.1	43.8

Table 2c Destination of school leavers by sex, England only, 1979

	% of boys	% of girls
Degree of Courses	8.7	6.0
Teacher Training	0.2	0.9
HND/HNC	0.4	0.3
OND/ONC	0.5	0.4
Catering	0.5	1.2
Nursing	—	1.5
Secretarial	—	4.8
'A' Levels	2.0	2.3
'O' Levels	1.3	1.7
Other Further Education Courses	3.6	6.7
Temporary Employment	0.9	0.7
Other Employment[1]	81.9	73.5
All Leavers	100.0	100.0

Note: [1]Including those whose destinations were not known

Source: *Education of girls: a statistical analysis,* Equal Opportunities Commission, 1981

Questions and activities

1 Using Tables 2a – 2c, list the general trends in girls' and boys' educational careers.
2 Using Table 2c and 2b, suggest which types of degree course might contain most women.
3 Suggest what types of skills most women might be learning on part-time courses.

Table 3   Women and mental illness

Most psychiatric symptoms are reported by women when they are at the time of life to be getting married, having babies and caring for their pre-school children at home alone. . . Hinkle and Wolf (1958) for example, found that there was a positive relationship between the amount of stress a woman reported and whether she was married with children, living in a nuclear family situation. Since the same relationship did not hold for

men, it seems that family life has particular strains for women.
Susan Lipshitz, 'Women and Psychiatry' in
The Sex Role System, Routledge and Kegan Paul, 1978

Table 3 *Admissions to mental illness hospitals and units by diagnostic group.*
England and Wales, 1975

ICD No.*	Diagnostic group	Males	Females
295, 297	Schizophrenia, schizo–affective disorders and paranoia	15,632	16,650
296	Depressive psychoses and involutional melancholia	7,314	16,723
291	Alcoholic psychosis	1,106	551
290	Senile and pre-senile dementia	3,126	7,186
292–294 298–299	} Other psychoses	5,282	8,699
300	Psychoneuroses	7,943	16,083
310–315	Mental handicap	496	478
303	Alcoholism	7,524	2,646
304	Drug dependence	1,161	602
301–302 306–308	} Personality and behaviour disorders	8,854	9,985
305, 309	Other psychiatric conditions	2,628	3,603
	All other undiagnosed cases and admissions for other than psychiatric disorders	14,561	27,248
	All diagnoses	75,627	110,454

* Internal Classification of Diseases, Injuries and Causes of Deaths, 1965 (Eighth Revision).

Source: Health and Personal Social Services Statistics, 1983

Questions and activities

1 What are the most common diagnoses for female patients? Suggest reasons for this.
2 Relate the evidence in this table with the findings summarised in Reading 5.
3 What are the particular stresses of the nuclear family situation? How might these be alleviated?

Table 4   Husband's participation in household tasks and childcare

The table below is from a survey of 175 working-class women who had returned to work following a period out of the workforce for childrearing. 90 per cent of the sample had children living at home.

1   Household Tasks (percentages)

	Cleaning	Shopping	Cooking	Washing-up	Washing	Gardening	Household repairs	Decorating
Never	25	43	27	17	61	27	15	18
Occasionally	38	22	38	35	18	26	35	15
Regularly	21	17	20	30	6	17	19	21
Always	3	4	2	5	2	16	15	32
No husband	14	14	14	14	14	14	14	14
	100	100	100	100	100	100	100	100

2   Childcare (percentages)

	Looks after children on his own	Puts children to bed on his own
Never	15	24
Occasionally	48	42
Regularly	37	35
	100	100

N= 146 relevant cases

Source: Equal Opportunities Research funded by Equal Opportunities Commission and SSRC, 1981

Questions and activities (Table 4)

1 Summarise the general trends shown in this table.
2 How might these trends differ in middle-class households?

Table 5   Reasons for working between first and second live births in four different time periods

Worked because	1956–60	1961–65	1966–70	1971–5
Really needed the money	52	51	48	47
Wanted extra things	27	25	27	27
Like it	16	19	20	22
Other reason	5	5	5	4

Source: Dunnell 1979, Table 6.5, p.31, reprinted in Oakley, *Subject Women*, Martin Robertson, 1981

Questions and activities (Table 5)

Identify the changes that have occurred in the reasons for women taking paid work between 1956 and 1975, and suggest reasons for these changes.

Questions and activities (Table 6)

Assess how this evidence could refute the claim of some social theorists that the primary division of the labour force is between manual and non-manual occupations. What other evidence would be needed to prove an argument against this claim?

Table 6   Earnings of male and female manual and non-manual workers 1983

Summary of results for full-time adults
Full-time men, aged 21 and over and full-time women aged 18 and over, whose pay for
the survey pay-period was not affected by absence

	Full-time men aged 21 and over			Full-time women aged 18 and over		
	Manual	Non-manual	All	Manual	Non-manual	All
Average gross weekly earnings	£143.6	£194.9	£167.5	£87.9	£115.1	£108.8
Average gross hourly earnings including overtime pay and overtime hours	326.5p	503.4p	399.1p	224.3p	310.0p	288.5p
excluding overtime pay and overtime hours	319.0p	502.9p	398.0p	222.0p	309.0p	287.5p

Source: *New Earnings Survey*, April 1983

Table 7 Occupational order for jobs of full and part-time working women and working men (1980 General Household Survey)

This table shows the occupations of women in full- and part-time paid work. The report from which this table was taken states: 'The concentration of the women into a relatively small number of occupations can be seen clearly. The three occupational orders with the highest proportions account for 69 per

Occupational order	Full time	Part-time	All working women	Working men (1980 GHS)
	(percentages)			
Managerial general	–	–	–	1
Professionals supporting management	2	0	1	6
Professionals in health, education and welfare	16	10	13	5
Literary, artistic and sports	1	1	1	1
Professionals in engineering and science	1	0	1	5
Other managerial	5	1	4	12
Clerical	41	22	33	6
Selling	6	13	9	4
Security	0	0	0	2
Catering, cleaning and hairdressing	10	41	23	3
Farming and fishing	1	2	1	2
Material processing (excluding metal)	1	1	1	3
Making and repairing (excluding metal)	6	4	5	6
Metal processing making, repairing	3	1	2	20
Painting, assembling, packing	6	3	5	5
Construction and mining	0	–	0	6
Transport	1	1	1	11
Miscellaneous	0	0	0	1
	100	100	100	100
Base	1,877	1,477	3,354	8,024

Source: *Women in Employment: a lifetime perspective*, Office of Population Census and Surveys 1984

cent of all women's jobs whereas four occupations have less than 1 per cent of women each. In contrast, the three orders with the highest proportions of men account for only 43 per cent of men's jobs and no occupation has less than 1 per cent of men.

Questions and activities

1 Discuss which types of skills might be found in the three occupational orders employing most women and the three occupational orders with the highest proportions of men.
2 How could the evidence in this table explain the failure of the Equal Pay Act to achieve equal pay for women?

Table 8   Changing composition of sex-segregated labour

This table shows the extent to which sex-typing of jobs has broken down this century. For example, in 1901, 47 per cent of all male workers worked in industries which employed no women at all. Only 11 per cent of female workers worked in women-only industries. By 1971, only 14 per cent of men worked in all-male industries but there were no all-female industries left. Murgatroyd argues that any erosion of sex-typing has therefore benefited men more than women.

	percentage of men working in occupations which had the following percentage of males					
	100	90+	80+	70+	60+	50+
1901	47	74	83	89	92	95
1971	14	53	69	77	84	87
	percentage of women working in occupations which had the following percentage of female workers					
	100	90+	80+	70+	60+	50+
1901	11	52	54	71	74	82
1971	0	25	44	51	75	77

Source: adapted from Hakim, 1979, in Linda Murgatroyd, *Gender and Occupational Stratification*, Lancaster Regional Group Working Paper 6, April, 1982

Questions and activities

Summarise the general trends shown in this table and discuss some of the female occupations into which men might have moved.

Table 9 G. P. Murdock and the division of labour by sex

On the basis of the data printed below, gathered from 224 societies, Murdock claimed that the division of labour by sex was universal and must, therefore, be advantageous to all societies. He believed men's 'superior' strength and women's physiological 'handicaps' to be reasons for the division. Close inspection of the data makes his claim appear somewhat exaggerated.

Table 9 Comparative data on the division of labour by sex

	Males only	Males frequently	Both	Females frequently	Females only	Per cent = degree of masculinity of a task
Weapon making	121	1	0	0	0	99.8
Hunting	166	13	0	0	0	98.2
Trapping or catching of small animals	128	13	4	1	2	94.9
Lumbering	104	4	3	1	6	92.2
Fishing	98	34	19	3	4	85.6
House building	86	32	25	3	14	77.0
Clearing of land for agriculture	73	22	17	5	13	76.3
Trade	51	28	20	8	7	73.7
Agriculture – preparation and planting	31	23	33	20	37	48.4
Erection/dismantling of shelter	14	2	5	6	22	39.8
Tending of fowls and small animals	21	4	8	1	39	38.7
Agriculture – crop tending and harvesting	10	15	35	39	44	33.9

Table 9 continued

	Males only	Males frequently	Both	Females frequently	Females only	Per cent = degree of masculinity of a task
Burden bearing	12	6	33	20	57	29.9
Preparation of drinks and narcotics	20	1	13	8	57	29.5
Gathering of fruits, berries and nuts	12	3	15	13	63	23.6
Cooking	5	1	9	28	158	8.6
Water carrying	7	0	5	7	119	8.2

Source: adapted from George P. Murdock, 'Comparative Data on the Division of Labour by Sex', *Social Forces* (October 1936 – May 1937), vol. 15, no.4, p. 552

Questions and activities (Table 9)

1 Using Murdock's evidence, assess his claim that women's 'physical handicaps' make them unsuited to particular types of work.
2 Assess the claim that women are most frequently employed in tasks which ensure the day to day survival of their social groups.

Questions and activities (Table 10)

1 In what ways may female subordination be functional to capital and in which ways may it be dysfunctional?
2 Describe some of the ways in which 'the ideology of femininity' may have changed in the last hundred years. Assess the degree to which such changes relate to economic factors.

Table 10 Current strands and unresolved problems of the socialist feminist debate on domestic labour women's oppressions as a result of:

1 Capitalism	2 Capitalism and patriarchy	3 Ideology
Women's oppression as a result of capitalist methods of production and reproduction.	Forged into one system?	Ideology about sex differences are cultural constructions, internalised within individuals.
Problem:	*Problem:*	*Problem?*
Not proven. Is privatised reproduction cheaper for capital?	Is patriarchy functional to capitalism? Not proven.	How do these constructions change over time?
How does this explain patriarchy in non-capitalist societies and within the working class, where the ownership of property is *not* a determinate of social relationships?	Two, parallel systems?	What factors – political, economic or ideological are most influential?
	Problem?	
	How did this arise? Are they mutually reinforcing or in conflict?	

Source: Adapted from Michele Barrett, *Women's Oppression Today*, Verso Edns, 1980

9 Documentary readings

Reading 1 Sex differences in the organisation of perception and cognition

This author makes two related points. First, that although there may be innate sex differences in intellectual function these are susceptible to improvement and second, that 'female' skills are frequently undervalued.

> Males begin with a female education in nearly every respect and their initial difficulties in reading and writing are well documented. . . The fact that boys do learn to read and write, as well as to speak fluently, suggests that though initial processes may be guided by certain sensory differences, there is no reason to assume that these differences must remain. Parents insist that boys learn to speak, read and write, but no such insistence induces the female to learn about spatial-mechanical relationships. . Spatial ability ought to be taught like speech and at an age which permits internalisation of processes by the time cognitive transformations occur. . . Without this help females will be disadvantaged at these sorts of tasks, and consistent failure becomes defeating.
>
> The evidence reviewed shows that females are communicative, and have a considerably greater interest in people than males have. . . females may be more sensitive to certain forms of emotional communication, possibly due to greater sensitivity to inflection. It would seem to me that sensitivity to people, 'social intelligence' is a trait which is profoundly important in maintaining a social system. Yet several authors imply that these female characteristics render them unable to carry out logical thought. . . statements of this type carry the implicit assumption that to be assertive, independent and unfeeling is good, but to have characteristics of sensitivity and co-operation is bad.

I would like to suggest that 'social intelligence', as yet entirely neglected by academic institutions, be given equal status with other forms of intellectual training. . . men and women are different. What needs to be made equal is the value placed upon these differences.

Diane McGuinness in *Exploring Sex Differences,*
Barbara Lloyd and John Archer (eds.),
Academic Press Inc., 1976

Questions and activities

1 In what ways do males 'begin with a female education in nearly every respect'?
2 Suggest ways in which spatial mechanical concepts could be taught in ways which girls might find relevant and interesting.
3 How is females' 'greater social intelligence' functional to social order and harmony?

Reading 2   Sexual divisions in the classroom

Stanworth studied A-level classes in a college of further education which offered, in theory at least, equality of opportunity to male and female students. She says: 'As the research proceeded, however, it became apparent that fairly subtle aspects of classroom encounters continued to regenerate a sexual hierarchy of worth, in which men emerged as the 'naturally' dominant sex.' This extract summarises her findings on the significance of gender in teachers' perceptions of their students:

The central concern of the study has been with the way in which, in pupil's experience, girls are placed on the margins of classroom encounters, and with the consequences this had for pupil's evolving images of the worth and capability of the sexes. . . When asked to pair those of their pupils who were, in some educationally relevant way, most alike, male teachers, unlike their female colleagues, show an overwhelming tendency to select same-sex pairs; they appear to be much more attuned to dissimilarity between the sexes than to qualities which girls and boys may have in common. This implicit tendency to perceive girls and boys as discrete groups may be translated into actions which polarise the girls and boys in the classes they teach; nearly all the pupils volunteer that these male teachers play on the division of the sexes in classroom discussion, and that they are substantially more sympathetic or more attentive to the boys than the girls.

All teachers – female as well as male – seem to be particularly responsive to the needs of male pupils. Teachers. . . more readily identify boys; when asked about first impressions of particular pupils, those who are reported as difficult to identify are, without exception, girls. . . Teachers. . . are also less likely, later in the year, to single out girls for positive emotional involvement. From amongst their many pupils, teachers of both sexes overwhelmingly chose boys as the pupils to whom they are most attached, and those for whom they are most concerned. . . it is their female pupils whom teachers most readily reject. . . [this] holds even when girls have a better academic record than the boys.

While teachers are concerned that neither girls nor boys should abandon their studies in order to get married or take a job, it is clear that teachers expect such disruptions more often in the case of their female pupils. Teachers have very different views of the futures awaiting their male and female pupils. Girls, even those with outstanding academic records, are expected to enter subordinate and conventionally feminine occupations, and, unlike boys, are seen as immersed in domestic commitments. Only when a girl's behaviour in class sharply contradicts the retiring feminine stereotype are her teachers likely to imagine her in a career at odds with highly traditional expectations.

Michelle Stanworth, *Gender and Schooling,*
Hutchinson, 1983

Questions and activities

1 Suggest ways in which 'the culture of masculinity' could be responsible for the increased attention given to boys in school.
2 Describe female behaviour which contributes to their being 'more difficult to identify' in classrooms.
3 What methods could be used to assess the qualitative and quantitative differences of treatment offered to male and female students?

Reading 3   The price of masculinity

This author argues that conformity to masculinity means rejection of all things feminine and, frequently, the adoption of an aggressively masculine image:

> Leslie Mapp observed that for men to adopt the expected male role and conform to society's notion of masculinity in our society comes at a cost. Men, he argued, pay a price for their privilege. This price includes 'the suppression of emotion, a predatory sexuality and a level of personal anxiety which demands continual competition to out-perform others'. Kate Myers commented that the traditional masculine values of taking as much pain as possible without giving in , being able to 'hold' alcohol, to show no feelings, to be competitive is hardly likely to fit in with equal participation in parenthood, with valuing women and respecting an equality of the sexes.
>
> According to psychologists such as Horney and Chodorow, boys learn to become men through a process of avoiding, even of coming to dread any association with the feminine. With an absent father, male children have no male model to copy, only their everpresent mother. The way of achieving masculinity becomes, therefore, a process of devaluing women, of rejecting female objects, activities, emotions, interests, etc. Boys learn to eschew the domestic and to repress the emotional side of life. Quoting the work of Margaret Mead, Chodorow aruges that maleness in our society is never absolutely defined. Unlike femininity, which in a patriarchal society is ascribed, masculinity and manhood has to be achieved, in a permanent process of struggle and confirmation.
>
> In this context it is hardly surprising that it is boys who are the most prone to construct and use gender categories. Not only do they have more at stake in such a system of classification (i.e. male power) but also they have to try to achieve manhood through the dual process of distancing women and femininity from themselves and maintaining the hierarchy and social superiority of masculinity by devaluing the female world.

Madeline Arnot, 'How Shall We Educate Our Sons?,
in *Co-Education Reconsidered,* Rosemary Deem (ed.),
Open University press, 1984

Questions and activities

1 Think of examples of the ways in which males reject and devalue femininity.
2 What is 'a predatory sexuality' and how does it compare with female sexuality?
3 In what ways is femininity 'ascribed' and masculinity 'achieved'?

Reading 4   The family as a quasi-feudal institution

The husband wife relationship can be understood as a quasi-feudal relationship in so far as the wife performs personal services for her husband in exchange for protection and goods. In many countries the husband is still required by law to support his wife. In exchange, either by law or by social custom, the wife is required to perform personal services for the husband which include sexual availability, maintenance of the household and care for the children, among others. Where there are laws which require that the wife's residence be where her husband's residence is, her mobility is restricted. She is required to move with him, if and when he moves, lest she be charged with desertion, and she may likewise not move into another residence unless she can persuade her husband to move with her. For her labour, the wife receives such goods as are necessary for her survival, namely shelter, food and clothes and according to circumstances, luxuries. The wife may therefore not be badly off but she has no right to a minimum wage, even though her husband may spend a lot of money on her. In other words, she may be expensively kept, but she is not even minimally paid. This is usually the case even though the wife may actually handle the major part of the family expenses. A financially dependent wife may spend money only under the constraint of a potential veto by her husband. For instance, if a wife decides that she is going to buy presents for her lover with the money that her husband gives her, the husband is quite likely to withdraw his money irrespective of the amount or the quality of labour performed by the wife. In other words, the wife does not have the power of disposing of the money in any way she sees fit. She only has as much control over purchases and expenditures as her husband is willing to grant her, and her control can be revoked for specific reason... her dependency echoes that of serf on lord.

Margrit Eichler, *The Double Standard: a feminist critique of feminist social science,* Croom Helm, 1980

Questions and activities

1 From the arguments presented in this reading, assess the claim that female emancipation will be achieved only when women are economically indepedent.
2 Find out which laws still assume and confirm women's economic dependence on men.

Reading 5   The sociology of housework

Oakley's sample was selected from the lists of two London GP's and comprised 20 working-class and 20 middle-class women. All were between the ages of twenty and thirty and all were married with at least one child. In addition to the findings summarised below, she found that the majority of women felt substantial identification with the role, and that middle-class women were more acutely conscious of the low status of housewifery and more critical of the work.

1 Dissatisfaction with housework predominates. Seventy per cent ... came out as 'dissatisfied'. .. during the course of a long in-depth interview.
2 Three-quarters of the sample report monotony and eighty per cent of these are dissatisfied with housework. Fragmentation... is also experienced by the majority... Excessive pace is reported by half the sample.
3 Loneliness is a frequent complaint. Most of the women who are dissatisfied with housework report a low level of social interaction with others...
4 Autonomy is the most highly valued dimension of the housewife role... [this] is a facet of housewifery which contrasts favourably with employment work.
5 Housework is the most disliked aspect of 'being a housewife'.
6 A perception of low status is related to housework dissatisfaction – more of those who complain about their status are

dissatisfied than satisfied.

7 The most liked tasks are (in order) cooking, shopping, washing, cleaning, washing up and ironing.

8 Housewives have a long working week. The average in this sample is 77 hours, with a range from 48 (the only housewife employed full time at the time of interview) to 105.

9 An important dimension of work behaviour is the felt need to specify standards and routines to which the housewife must adhere in the course of work performance. . . [it is] a means of creating unity out of a collection of heterogeneous work tasks. Secondly, it is a way of expressing the feeling of personal responsibility for housework. Thirdly, it establishes a means of obtaining reward in housework – satisfaction can be gained daily from successful adherence to these standards and routines. . .

10 By attaining the standards and repeating the routines they set themselves, women may be able to gain a measure of psychological satisfaction. . . failure to achieve one's pre-set goals may bring about substantial dissatisfaction.

11 Dissatisfaction with housework is higher among those who report work satisfaction in a previous job; in the women's comments housework is unfavourably compared with employment work, which, whatever the particular nature of the work, offers company, social recognition and financial reward.

Ann Oakley, *The Sociology of Housework,*
Martin Robertson, 1974

Questions and activities

1 Discuss the ways in which Oakley's findings might form the basis of large-scale research into women's attitudes to housework.

2 Compare and contrast the findings here with a summary of research into factory life, e.g. Beynon's *Working for Ford,* Allen Lane, 1973.

3 Explain why only a long in-depth interview revealed the respondents' dissatisfaction with housework.

Reading 6   Shared child care

In this reading the author describes child-care in one pre-developed society and compares it with the more isolated child-rearing practices in Western cultures:

> The Kgatla baby is under the care and supervision of a sister or cousin from the age of a few months until it is weaned. . . . The baby is part of the community from the word go, whereas so many babies in advanced societies spend their first months cocooned in a pram. . . their view . . . interrupted from time to time only by the face of the mother looking down. The Kgatla mother was liberated to get on with her own affairs while the little girls were learning. . . the vital if not always welcome lessons of responsibility and co-operation. . . . There are very few primitive societies where baby-care isolates the infants from its human environment in the way it so often does in the West.
>
> Clarke and Hindley, *The Challenge of the Primitive*, Cape, 1975

Reading 7   Participative fathering

This extract reviews some of the research into participative fathering and outlines the implications for social policy if it is to enable childrearing to be shared between women and men.

> As men become more fully involved with family, they no longer see their primary role as breadwinner, but also as husband and father. This is shown by the fact that growing numbers of men are attending childbirth, supporting wives in the post-natal period, and involving themselves in childrearing. . .
>
> Pleck (1979) sums up the changing roles of both mothers and fathers: 'An increased family role is the single most important manifestation of change in the male role in contemporary society, just as increased labour force participation is probably the most important change in female role.'
>
> The growing involvement of fathers in family life produces its own strains between family and working life. . .
>
> Pleck (1980) explored the specific job characteristics that caused or exacerbated the tension between work and family lives. Husbands and wives reported the following characteris-

tics to be most significantly associated with the work-family conflict: frequent overtime, the work schedule, and physically and psychologically demanding work. . .

Elliot (1978) investigated the consequence of heavy work commitments for fathers' role performance among middle-class families. It was reported that fathers felt themselves to be shadow figures in the background of their families. Fathers of young children often felt that their children scarcely seemed to recognise them, while fathers of older children perceived themselves to be remote figures on the periphery of their children's lives. The wives also reported negative consequences for both themselves and their children as a result of their husbands heavy involvement in their work.

One argument that recurs is that equal opportunities for both parents to fully and satisfactorily enact their roles in both the family and work situation will only be ensured through comprehensive governmental social policies concerning the family. Traditionally, family policy has been viewed primarily as a women's issue – fathers are considered as economic support for the family – but the actual focus of the policies are geared to the protection of women and children. To be effective, however, family policies must consider the total family and parental roles of men as well as women.

Colin Bell, Lorna McKee, and Karen Priestly,
Fathers, Childbirth and Work, EOC, 1983

Questions and activities

1 Which social classes are most likely to experience the tensions described by Pleck?
2 By referring to Table 5, assess the claim made in the first paragraph of this reading.
3 What social policies would enable increased participative fathering?

Reading 8   Managerial myths about women

These extracts are from a paper which reviews research into managerial attitudes toward women workers. Much of this work has exposed stereotypical attitudes among those in a position to hire and promote women. The author describes these as 'myths' and offers evidence to refute them:

1 *Workers do not like working for a woman manager*
These managerial judgements do not stand up to the evidence.
In one survey three quarters of the male and female executives
who had worked with women managers reacted favourably.

2 *Women are less dependable*
Evidence from this country and the USA indicates the following about turnover: higher turnover rates are true of all
employees, irrespective of sex, who are under 25 and are in
low-income clerical jobs.

3 *Women are financially dependent on men*
Land (1975) quotes census figures which show that, in Britain,
'nearly two million women under retirement age are the chief
economic supporters of their households' and that 'the majority of these households contain either children or adult dependents, including husbands'. Furthermore, '. . . the number of
two parent families having incomes at or below supplementary benefit scale rates would have trebled if earnings
by the mother had not been combined with those of the
father'.

5 *Women will only work until they marry*
Married women make up the majority of working women and
are increasing as a proportion of the workforce. (Department
of Employment 1974; OECD 1975). 'A majority of working
women be they single or married' would positively prefer to
be in paid employment.

6 *Children are damaged by having working mothers*
The most recent evidence indicates that child studies have
confounded separation with deprivation and that bond disruption is not a necessary consequence of separation. (Rutter,
1972; National Child Development Study, 1972; Baruch, 1972;
Arnott, 1972.)
        Oonagh Hartnett, *The Sex Role System,* Routledge, 1978

Questions and activities

1 Using the evidence in section 2 of this reading and the
evidence in Table 8, explain why it may appear that 'women
are less dependable'.
2 Describe how 'maternal separation' is not necessarily the same
thing as 'maternal deprivation'.

Reading 9   Trade union's exclusionary policies

This reading provides some historical explanation for the failure of trade unions to protect women workers. The author claims that trade union apathy, even hostility, to women workers until the 1960s provides reason for women's lack of trade union activity today and for their poor barganing position in the workforce. She sees industrialisation as a source of conflict between the sexes:

Here we see for the first time the economic interests of women brought into conflict with those of men. There followed throughout the first half of the nineteenth century a stout rearguard action by male workers, in which two of the main weapons were machine wrecking and the trade union. Women workers had become an extension of the bosses self-interest and therefore victims rather than beneficiaries of trade union militancy. The faster the pace of technological improvement, the faster were machines able to break down complex operations thus allowing in even more women workers and stiffening male trade unionist's resolve to make life awkward for them. In 1975, for example, the Manchester Spinners Society allowed women into membership. But when, in 1829, a Grand General Union of Spinners in the United Kingdom was formed, a resolution was adopted that, 'the union shall include only male spinners and piecers'.

In Scotland there were bitter struggles to keep out underpaid, under-organised women and children from spinning rooms. Earlier, women and children had only been used in the textile mills in areas where there was a shortage of men; now they were being preferred to men. Had trade unionism been allowed to develop freely as the last century began, men workers might have been able to absorb women into their unions, and to use their combined strength to stop employers from undercutting male wage rates... On repeal of the Combination Acts, many weaving unions voted to exclude women, and it is from then on that the principle of two separate labour markets, one for men and one for women was institutionalised as a fact of British industrial life.

Until a century after the first Trades Union Congress, held in 1868, trade unionists rarely took women workers and their problems seriously; when they did it was to see female employment as a threat to the interests of male workers. . . Not until 1968 did equal pay become a serious political issue, that being the year that a Labour government produced proposals for legislation. The TUC threw its weight behind the proposals, supporting a tougher Act than actually got on to the Statute Book.

Ross Davies, *Women and Work*, **Arrow Books, 1975**

Questions and activities

1 From the evidence in this passage evaluate the claim that industrialisation divided the working class on sex-lines.
2 In what ways did women workers become 'an extension of the bosses self interest'?

Reading 10   Women in trade unions

This study surveyed 175 women who had returned to work since 1970. It found: 'Lack of trade union at the place of work was a most reliable predictor of low pay. . . Predictably, low pay was associated with working in service industries, domestic work, food preparation and with small firms'.

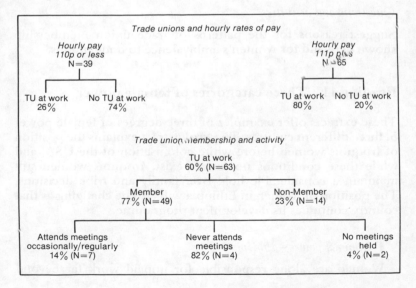

Trade union membership is higher than the stereotype of the married woman worker would suggest with a high percentage of those who have a union at their place of work actually joining. Most women said that they joined the union because it was a closed shop or 'everybody does' and explained their non-attendance at meetings by their part-time status. Either they were never at work when meetings were held or 'the union isn't really for part-timers'. They were not anti-union (this sample included three shop stewards) but their comments were ambivalent. On the one hand they believed in the principal of solidarity, it wasn't right not to join when every-one else did; on the other hand very few thought that unions were really very relevent to women workers. This was a very specific instance of the general acceptance of the sexual division of labour. Working entails entering a male sphere of interest (even when that work is within the ghetto of married women's employment) and the women held few expectations that the established institutions of that sphere would serve their own interest.

Judith Chaney, *Social Networks and Job Information; the situation of women who return to work,* EOC/SSRC, 1981

Questions and activities

Suggest reasons for the patterns of trade union membership shown here and for women's ambivalence to trade unions.

Reading 11   Three categories of female power

These extracts offer examples of three degrees of female power in three different cultures. The final extract explains the position of Iroquois women before white colonisation of the USA, and while these conditions no longer exist, Iroquois women still maintain a considerable hold over family and tribe decisions. The position of women in Ethiopia will also be changing as that country continues its development programme.

1 *Minimal power – Ethiopia*

Women are alone responsible for unpaid work far beyond

childcare and household work. A typical peasant woman rises at 5 a.m. to do household chores before her day's work in the fields while watching the children. All that she produces in the fields is expropriated by her husband and/or landlord. Later she returns home to cook dinner (always eating last herself), wash her husband's feet, put him and the children to bed, and do more household chores. . .

The little paid work available includes gathering and selling wood, carrying water, cooking and cleaning for wealthy families, working in low-level factory jobs and prostitution.

2 Token power – Sweden

[Legislation] . . . helps free women to take part in the paid labour force, which has been short of skilled labour, and makes it easier for women to have children. Although the current proposed changes are increasing women's status, they are being initiated by a male-dominated government that could deny these rights as fast as they are being given. . . Women's fertility has been given great support through many social programs from extensive maternity benefits to family allowances, including single mothers, and increasing though still inadequate childcare facilities. The government has also run a campaign encouraging men to share parental duties and care of the home. . . It is true that men must be doing housework and childcare before women can reach all their goals in other areas, but it is sometimes assumed that men will sacrifice their privileges voluntarily, with encouragement. The vast majority of men in Sweden haven't. . . Women still do not have full economic independence, nor the social independence to define their futures for themselves. . .

3 Negotiating power – The Iroquois

Iroquois women presided over the residences and the long-houses, and ultimate authority over the household was held by the matron (an older woman chosen by all the women). The matrons selected the male council of elders, deposed them if they behaved inappropriately, and influenced their decisions. . . Work groups of women were responsible for the planting and cultivating of the fields and the harvest, though sometimes the men helped them. They also gathered food and fished. . . and sometimes went on hunting expeditions with the men. . . Marriages were arranged by the mothers of the concerned persons and either husband or wife could obtain a divorce with little ceremony. . . Women also controlled most of the wealth of the clan in the form of stored food.

Lisa Leghorn and Katherine Parker, *Woman's Worth,*
Routledge and Kegan Paul, 1981

Questions and activities

1 Using this reading and the views expressed in Reading 15, discuss why patriarchy is a difficult concept to define.
2 Why did the negotiating power of Iroquois women diminish with the impact of European settlers in the United States?
3 Explain why Leghorn and Parker might be less than satisfied with legislation that gives women token power?

Reading 12   Is female to male as nature is to culture?

In the paper from which these extracts were taken, Ortner claims that the 'pancultural fact' of women's subordination can be explained by the drive to control and 'tame' natural forces:

My thesis is that woman is being identified with . . . seems to be a symbol of – something that every culture devalues, something that every culture defines as being of a lower order of existence than itself.

And that is 'nature'. . . Every culture, or generically 'culture', is engaged in the process of generating and sustaining systems of meaningful forms (symbols, artifacts etc) by means of which humanity transcends the givens of natural existence, bends them to its purposes, controls them in its interest. . . humanity attempts to assert control over nature. . . [women's] pancultural second-class status could be accounted for, quite simply, by postulating that women are being identified or symbolically associated with nature, as opposed to men who are identified with culture. Since it is always culture's project to subsume and transcend nature, if women were considered part of nature, then culture would find it 'natural' to subordinate, not to say oppress them. . . . It all begins of course with the body and the natural procreative functions specific to women alone. . . Woman's body and its functions, more involved more of the time with 'species life' seem to place her closer to nature, in contrast to man's physiology, which frees him more completely to take up the projects of culture. . . It is simply a fact that proportionately more of woman's body space, for a greater percentage of her lifetime. . . is taken up with the natural processes surrounding the reproduction of the species. . . In other words, woman's body seems to doom her to mere reproduction of life; the male in contrast, lacking natural creative functions, must (or has the opportunity to) assert his creativity externally, 'artificially', through the medium of technology and symbols. In so doing, he creates relatively lasting, external, transcendent objects, while the woman creates only perishables – human beings.

It is hardly contestable that the domestic is always subsumed by the public. . . society. . . is logically at a higher level than the domestic units of which it is composed. . . since women are associated with, and indeed are more or less confined to, this domestic context, they are identified with this lower order of social/cultural organisation. . . and hence, so the cultural reasoning seems to go, men are the 'natural' proprietors of religion, ritual, politics, and other realms of cultural thought and action.

Sherry B. Ortner in *Feminist Studies* vol.1, no.2, Maryland, 1972

Questions and activities

1 What particular features of female life might lead to their being seen as 'closer to nature'?

2 In what ways are womens' reproductive functions devalued or demeaned in Western societies?

3 Why might Ortner be accused of 'biological determinism' from the evidence presented in this extract?

Reading 13 I call myself a radical feminist

It [radical feminism] is a recognition that no single element of our society has evolved free from male definition, so that to practice radical feminism means to question every single aspect of our lives that we have previously accepted as normal/ given/ standard/ acceptable and to find new ways of doing things where necessary – which is most places. Thus, language is male defined. This does not mean that some women have not become very good at using it, but that the language as presently constructed is based on male-dominated values, since patriarchy was in control long before Saxon times. . . until radical feminism told many women that there were important concepts missing from our thought patterns/ language, and that this was yet another weapon in the armoury of male oppression, many women thought/felt that they were stupid, inarticulate, inferior for not having the words to describe the conditions of their being.

Others of us have looked at other areas of our previously taken-for-granted existence, such as believing that some people know more about some things, and therefore we call them experts and pay them higher wages and don't answer back when they tell us things about ourselves that we know are wrong. Remember that many of these experts are men. Radical feminism told us it was possible to take on the man, especially if we do it collectively, and win. We also discovered that a lot of the information of these so-called experts that was valuable to us could be learned fairly easily, once we gained confidence in our ability to do it. Concepts such as 'knowledge', 'science', 'rationality' are being constantly reassessed. . . Marx said a lot of very important things but, like us all, he was a product of his milieu – a nineteenth century, urban, Western European, Jewish, intellectual man. All these things, and more, led him to make assertions incorrect for achieving a twentieth-century and/or rural and/or non-European and/or feminist revolution.

Gail Chester in *Feminist Practice: notes from the tenth year*,
London, In Theory Press, 1979

Questions and activities

1 Suggest ways in which language may be seen as 'male defined' and relate this to Friedan's discovery of 'the problem without a name' (p.33), and to the evidence presented in Table 4.
2 Research the ways in which some men have become 'experts'

in spheres which were once considered to be female work. e.g. childbirth. Discuss the impact of this on women's lives.

3 How could concepts such as 'knowledge, science and rationality' be reassessed from a feminist perspective? What could be the impact of such reassessment on education?

4 From your knowledge of the work of Marx, and of later Marxist theory, work out what may be the 'incorrect assertions' to which Gail Chester refers.

Reading 14 Universals and particulars in the position of women

This extract is from a paper in which Penelope Brown discusses the problems of trying to use the blanket term 'patriarchy' as a feature of women's secondary status. She argues that definitions of femininity vary so much between cultures that we must incorporate this fact into analysis.

Neither the 'position of women' nor 'patriarchy' are simple and self-evident concepts. . . In my view, explanations for the status of women are in a primitive state, for we have not yet learned to pose the questions we are asking in a form precise enough to allow meaningful answers. . . Simple economic determinist explanations don't work, because. . . women do the major productive labour in some societies, and yet are still subordinate (by some criteria) to men. It is quite possible to control food production almost entirely and still be largely left out of the society's political and ritual activities, or be required (at least within their own social stratum) to give public deference to men. Even in modern socialist countries, there has apparently been great resistance to changing the allocation to women of the primary responsibility for housework and childcare.

Other key explanations don't seem to work any better than economic ones – they frequently conflict with the data, and they are in any case too general to be of much use in understanding the particular forms of sexual oppression. We are left with some puzzles about very general cross-cultural patterns: the monopoly of men over formal political office; the exclusion of women from prestige spheres; ideologies of sex difference favouring men.

There is no 'objective', cross-culturally valid, criterion for evaluating the position of women... women are socially constructed. If we take this position seriously, then it means that the notion of 'woman' has to be interpreted *within* the parameters and definitions meaningful to the society that does the constructing. There is no essence of woman distinct from the definition of 'woman' within a society, and if a theory of patriarchy is to be developed which doesn't fly in the face of ethnographic fact, it will have to confront the variety and complexity of such definitions of 'woman' with a great deal of subtlety and sensitivity.

Penelope Brown in *Women in Society: interdisciplinary essays,*
Virago, 1981

Bibliography

Barret, Michele, *Women's Oppression Today*, Verso Edns, 1980.
  Through examination of the key issues of female subordina-
  tion, Barrett discusses the problems of achieving a Marxist/
  Feminist synthesis. A demanding book for A-level students
  but repays careful reading.
Eichler, Margrit, *The Double Standard: a feminist critique of feminist
  social science*, Croom Helm, 1980.
  Eichler explodes many of the 'myths' of sociological analysis
  of women, including some offered by feminist academics.
  Good section on women and class analysis.
Evans, Mary (ed.), *The Woman Question*, Fontana, 1982.
  Selection of readings from classic texts as well as from recent
  work in Britain and America. Sound, introductory material
  providing excellent background reading on a very wide variety
  of issues.
Illich, Ivan, *Gender*, Marion Boyars, 1983.
  This book is not easy reading but will prove useful for teachers
  wanting material on the effects of capitalist development on
  sex role. As well as his exposition, Illich's footnotes provide a
  wealth of evidence and references.
Laws, Judith Long, *The Second X: sex role and social role*, Elsevier,
  New York, 1979.
  Explores the construction of femininity from childhood onwards through to a section on 'a feminist future'. Refers to the
  intellectual double standard of male scholarship. Good reference material.
Leghorn, Lisa, and Parker, Katherine, *Woman's Worth: sexual
  economics and the world of women*, Routledge and Kegan Paul, 1981.
  A wide range of cross-cultural studies exploring economic
  influences on women's lives, especially those hitherto ignored
  by traditional economics. Particularly useful for introducing
  the effects of development on women's lives. A scholarly work
  which uses song, poetry and conversation to describe women's
  experience. Students will enjoy this book.

Oakley, Ann, *Subject Women,* Martin Robertson, 1981.
 Probably still the best introductory work to the debate. Oakley
 draws upon an impressive range of empirical work and her
 style is lively and accessible to students new to sociology.
Roberts, Helen, (ed.), *Doing Feminist Research,* Routledge and
Kegan Paul, 1981.
 Starting from the premise that women have largely been
 ignored in the study of social processes, this selection of
 readings introduces students to the ways in which making
 women 'visible' might affect the research process.
Spender, Dale, *Invisible Women: the schooling scandal,* Writers and
Readers Publishing Co-operative, 1982.
 A lively discussion on the central issues concerning women
 and education. Spender's polemical style should encourage
 students to read more widely and she gives excellent references and sources for further study.
Women's Studies Group, *Women Take Issue: aspects of women's
subordination,* Hutchinson, 1978.
 A collection of readings which combine theoretical work and
 contemporary case studies to explore the material and ideological base of women's inequality. Most readings suitable for
 good A-level students.

Further References

As stated in the introduction, this text has not covered in detail
the ways in which mass media, religion and the law have
reflected and reinforced male dominance. The following texts
may provide introductory readings.

Law

Coussins, J., *The Equality Report,* National Council for Civil
Liberties, Rights for Women Unit, London, 1976.
 Aspects of the legal status of women and their treatment
 before the law.

Media

King, J., and Stott, M., (eds.), *Is This Your Life? images of women in the media,* Virago, London, 1977.
    A simple, introductory text useful for students of all abilities.

Religion

Reuther, Rosemary Radford, (ed.), *Religion and Sexism: images of women in the Jewish and Christian traditions,* Touchstone, 1974.
    A selection of essays relating patriarchal religion and the ideology of femininity.

Index